Gods & Vampires

Gods & Vampires

RETURN TO CHIPAYA

Nathan Wachtel

Translated by Carol Volk

THE UNIVERSITY OF CHICAGO PRESS

Chicago and London

NATHAN WACHTEL is professor of history and the anthropology
of Meso- and South American Societies at the Collège de France.

The University of Chicago Press, Chicago 60637
The University of Chicago Press, Ltd., London
© 1994 by The University of Chicago
All rights reserved. Published 1994
Printed in the United States of America

03 02 01 00 99 98 97 96 95 94   1 2 3 4 5
ISBN: 0-226-86763-3 (cloth)
        0-226-86764-1 (paper)

Originally published in Paris as *Dieux et vampires: Retour à
Chipaya*, ©Editions du Seuil, 1992. La Librairie du XXᵉ siècle,
sous la direction de Maurice Olender.

Library of Congress Cataloging-in-Publication Data

Wachtel, Nathan.
    [Dieux et vampires. English]
    Gods and vampires : return to Chipaya / Nathan Wachtel ;
translated by Carol Volk.
        p.   cm.
    Includes bibliographical references and index.
    1. Chipaya Indians—Social life and customs.   2. Social
structure—Bolivia—Chipaya.   3. Social change—Bolivia—
Chipaya.   4. Ethnology—Bolivia—Chipaya—Field work.
5. Chipaya (Bolivia)—Social conditions.   I. Title.
F2520.1.C6W3213   1994
984'.00498—dc20   93-35865
                                                        CIP

For Martin Quispe

Contents

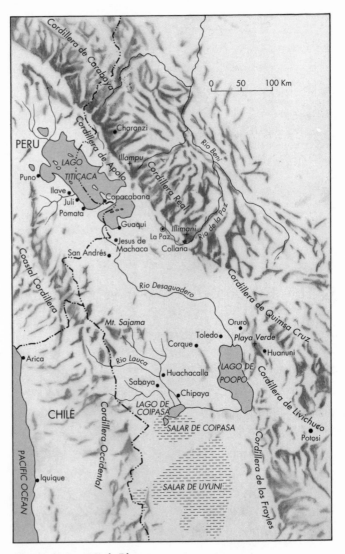

The Bolivian High Plateau

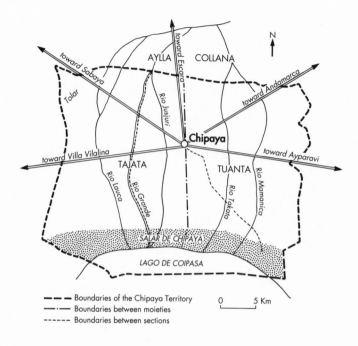

The Chipaya Territory

Yesterday and Today

OCTOBER 1989: AFTER SEVEN YEARS OF ABSENCE, I am back in Chipaya. Sixteen years have passed since my first visit. On the horizon, to the west, loom the massive silhouette of the Tata Sabaya volcano and the snowy peaks of the Andes, while around us the vegetation grows thinner and thinner: the bushy tufts vanish once the van passes Escara. Now, with the sun directly overhead, I can see the bare, white pampa glisten, its flatness broken only by the mossy mounds scattered among the salt patches. In the distance, something golden flashes intermittently—a jeep coming from the other direction. When we reach the ford of the Lauca river, the vehicle stops. I glance inside: at the wheel is a bearded man I've never met, and in the back, amid all the baggage and parcels, whom should I see but Santiago Condori, surprised and smiling, who has also recognized me, the very Santiago whose story concludes *Le Retour des ancêtres*[1] and who, by a very strange coincidence and without meaning to, has come to meet me! His decision is made in an instant: he collects his bundles, climbs out of the jeep (to the amazement of his driver), and returns to Chipaya with me. As a result, I take up lodgings in the same house as during my previous visit.

In the late afternoon, I wander through the village, which only vaguely resembles the one I knew in the past. In the 1970s, Chipaya could still be distinguished from the other villages of the high plateaus by its round, straw-covered huts, similar to those in the early-seventeenth-century drawings of the chronicler Guaman Poma de Ayala. They were grouped in each moiety in seemingly chaotic clusters, and it was difficult to make out the four "streets" that, according to the municipal agent in 1973 (who even then was Santiago Condori), extended from the main square to the four corners. I remember how amused and surprised I felt at the lofty names he used to designate them, pointing with his finger at very vague plots of land. "You see, this is Bolivar Street, this is Sucre Street!" As I attempt to recall the vanished landscape, I notice that almost all the houses are now built according to a rectangular plan, arranged in docile alignment on either side of wide sandy paths. Some even have corrugated metal roofs. The few round huts that remain, buried among all the new homes, seem to be falling into decay. As everywhere else on the high plateau, a certain modernity has engulfed the village: it's Chipaya and yet it's no longer Chipaya.

I discover one innovation that I particularly appreciate: with the help of the CORDEOR (the "Oruro Development Corporation"), the Chipaya have channeled the Lauca river and for the past year have had running water. No more lugging muddy, brackish water from the wells! Now each patio is equipped with that miracle of civilization, a faucet. To the east of the village, facing Manasaya, stands a hideous little cement tower that maintains a reservoir and houses a motor; although in a contrasting style, it provides a kind of balance to the church steeple. The evening of my arrival, some friends who came to visit recount with pride and amusement the vicissitudes of the tower's construction: armed with their scientific knowledge, the engineers from the CORDEOR at first ignored the advice of the Chipayas, which cost them repeated failures. Only when they finally followed the advice of the indigenous people did their work meet with success.

Among my visitors, I have the pleasure of seeing Martin, my best informant and friend, who for many years has shared with me his prodigious knowledge in matters of customs and oral traditions. Reserved and a little awkward, he speaks in carefully balanced phrases infused with subtle humor. He is wearing what seems to be the style among many Chipayas: an ugly Korean-made cap, with a wide, bright-red visor. Since he speaks with his head down, his face immersed in the shadow of the dim candlelight, only his thin, nasal voice emerges from the visor. With him is his brother Juan, who looks emaciated: he explains that he has just returned from the lowlands of Chaparé, where he attempted to establish himself as a colonist farmer; he couldn't stand the tropical climate and decided to return to the village. That same evening, a minor event teaches me that I have to relearn certain small differences. Knowing Martin's love of dictionaries, I have brought him a handsome encyclopedia as a present. Without thinking, following our own customs, I have brought it gift-wrapped, tied with a beautiful ribbon. This was tactless of me: Martin turns the object over and over in his hands, disconcerted. No matter how strongly I urge him, he doesn't dare open it. Finally I open it myself. Delighted and intimidated, he leafs through the glossy pages of the book.

After my friends leave, I allow myself to wander through the village one more time: under the starry sky, in the diffused light of the crescent moon, it begins to look just as strange and eerie as it did years ago. The recent transformations are erased, the most distant past now seems to overpower the present. The reflections of pale patches of wall cut through the formless mass of areas submerged in blackness, while the extraordinary sharpness of my shadow on the ground makes me feel like a *chullpa*

myself, walking silently through this village of
chullpas, beings who, according to the creation
myth, inhabited the earth before the appearance of
the sun. When the sun came out, all the *chullpas*
were destroyed, consumed by the celestial fire, ex-
cept for the few who took refuge in lakes; the Chipayas, along with the other Urus, are the
descendants of these survivors of the first "judg-
ment." They are the last witnesses in this world to a
primeval humanity. Hence the disdain of their
neighbors, the Aymara Indians, who call them
chullpa-puchu or "rejects" from the pre-solar age,
excluded from mankind today.

Over the next few days I continue my exploration,
struggling to relearn the layout of the village. For although I was able to find almost all of my friends,
many of them have built new homes and I don't
know where they live anymore. Families continue to
cluster in the same neighborhoods, but so many
changes have occurred in the distribution of dwell-
ings (in particular, young couples settling in) that I
am forced to establish new reference points as if I
were in a city where I'd never been before. In Aransaya, for instance, I search in vain for the chapel of
the moiety, which is dedicated to Santiago. What
surprises me is not so much that I can't find it, but

that I can't even identify its former location. The same thing happens in Manasaya, with the chapel of San Gerónimo. I wait several days before asking friends to direct me, only to discover that greenhouses have replaced the old chapels; onions and carrots are now being cultivated there. This innovation was introduced recently with the help of the official CORDEOR. But why did the Chipayas choose these sites, which in theory are sacred, for this entirely prosaic garden? This must be a consequence of the religious conflicts that have been dividing the village for the past twenty years.

Another sign of modernization: the school, which was like a village within a village, has been expanded considerably, to the point of impinging on the former soccer field. Even in the 1970s the school of Chipaya offered the full cycle of primary education. Now students can pursue a secondary education, since the creation in 1985 of a junior high school baptized "Uru Andino." It's a regular campus, occupying a vast expanse to the north of the village. Due to accelerating population growth, youth are in the majority in Chipaya: hence the rhythms of daily life are dominated by the rhythms of school life, making this desolate pampa in the high plateaus feel almost like a college town. The background noise, which was familiar to me, seems even more animated than before: the sound of children running to school in the early morning, the bell marking the end of class, the piercing screams and laughter during recreation, the national anthem sung at the beginning and end of the school day, and the commotion once school is out. The noise of the boisterous young students is now accompanied by the calmer sounds of the junior high schoolers, who in the late afternoon (at least when the strong wind doesn't force them to stay home) gather around the square to talk in small groups. The boys are generally dressed in Western-style clothing while the girls continue to wear the traditional black tunic. And in what is perhaps a sign of the changing times, scenes of romance appear to be more frequent: on either side of a low wall, a young man, sitting on his bicycle, and a young girl, standing on her patio, converse affectionately in hushed tones.

§

Has Chipaya become just like the other villages? The holiday of October 12 (*"Dia de la raza"*),[2] celebrated everywhere else in Boliva, used to be unknown here. It was recently introduced by the teachers to commemorate both the creation of the junior high school and that of the "fifth section" of the province of Atahuallpa, composed of the Chi-

paya and Ayparavi cantons (with the village of Chipaya as its seat—a position of great distinction). As
is customary, the festivities begin the night before. A
torch parade is scheduled; on the square, facing the
authorities, who are bearing *varas* (command staffs)
and dressed in their traditional costumes, a young
student recites a congratulatory speech, which is enthusiastically applauded. In the clear, cold night,
under the full moon, the other-worldliness of the
lanterns and dancing shadows reminds me of the national holiday I attended in 1973 in the neighboring
village of Huachacalla. The cortege moves in front of
the administrative office of the *corregidor;* everyone
warms up before a wood fire, stomping their feet,
the rising wind sending sparks into the air. A very
"Bolivian" picture in its austere beauty, like certain
scenes in *The Courage of the People,* the film by
Sanjines. Martin leads me to a warmer office, where
we huddle together. I am surprised to see several
cups of liquor circulating, as at celebrations in the
past. Sitting to my right, a jovial truck driver with a
mustache, from Coipasa, seems to be thoroughly enjoying the pleasures of the late night activity. The
deafening brass orchestra strikes up in this narrow
refuge: I take advantage of the commotion to slip
away.

The next morning when I head toward the square,

everyone is gathering in a semicircle opposite the au-

thorities, who are lined up to form a "tribunal," still
in front of the *corregidor*'s office. The empty space in
the middle serves as a stage on which a theatrical
program is being performed, punctuated by pro-
nouncements (by the teachers) in the guise of inter-
ludes. First the schoolchildren, awkwardly but with
great determination, present a few sketches or short
comedies; then four women, members of the "Society of Mothers," with hats and layered skirts, act out
comic market scenes, which have the crowd in
stitches. I draw closer to follow the stories better and
run into the bearded man I met the first day at the
wheel of the jeep: he's the priest of Chipaya, who has
been living for the past five years in the village
(which never in the course of its history had a resident priest). We greet each other politely, but I sense
a certain reserve in his overly respectful manner (he
calls me "Professor" every time he addresses me). Is
it a trick question when he asks: "Some people regret that the Chipayas are becoming more like the
Aymaras. What do you think, Professor?" I respond
with carefully balanced comments on respect for
cultural identities and the ineluctable course of history. He seems surprised by the nuance I take pains
to express. Right in front of us, the contrast is striking between the younger students, dressed in tradi-

tional outfits, and the older ones wearing school
uniforms: a white smock for the girls and blue trousers and shirts for the boys.

Our conversation is interrupted by the next event
on the program: it's time for the parade. The entire
population lines up on the other side of the square,
the authorities and leading citizens in front carrying
banners and Bolivian flags, followed, in separate
groups, by the men, the women, the elementary
school students, the junior high students, the teachers (among whom the priest takes his place), and finally the brass band, blasting out a military march.
In the first row I notice Martin walking proudly, his
head held high, carefully following the step: Is he
proud of being placed among the leading citizens or,
like all other Chipayas on this special holiday, of at-
taining the dignity of citizen status? After a half-turn
around the square, the authorities stop to form another tribunal on the western side, while the other
groups continue to parade before them. The largest
group is that of the schoolchildren and junior high
students. The oldest among them stand out: wearing tall, peaked caps, they play and dance as if at the
Oruro Carnival. Since the whole village is participating in the parade (or is gathered with the tribunal), the truck driver and I, lost in the middle of the
large square, are among the few spectators. The en-

tire scene seems both absurd and moving, ordinary
and strange: I know that the same parade is taking
place everywhere, in every Bolivian village, but it is
surprising to see it here for the first time. Is this,
then, modern Chipaya? Continuing, in my mind, the
conversation with the priest, I catch myself arguing,
"After all, why shouldn't the Chipayas have the
same right as everyone else to be ordinary? Why
shouldn't they be citizens like everyone else?"

§

I know from experience that the first week of a visit
is spent seeing old friends, and that my presence inevitably disturbs village routines: a certain amount
of time has to pass for things to settle down. The
truth is, I am not planning to work as intensively as I
did before; this time I'm simply paying a friendly
visit. I have just finished my major work on the Urus,
and it would seem wrong to publish it without paying tribute to my Chipaya hosts now that it has been
written. Rereading my notebooks from the 1970s,
I'm surprised at how I would continue my inquiries
for days at a time during my previous visits, speaking to a string of interlocutors, one after the other,
without stopping, from early morning until late at
night. Now I can accept the idea of spending long,
empty hours strolling through the nearly deserted

village, without systematically trying to "pick up" possible informants. And even if it means interrupting an interview, I never fail to head to the outskirts of Aransaya in the late afternoon to contemplate the sunset, whose colors, because of the transparency of the air at this altitude, have an unreal quality, changing shades at every instant, from gold to orange to a burst of flaming purple. More moving still, this spectacle is mirrored in the sparkling water of the canals, where the silver reflections blend with the shimmer of the skies—a play of colors that is unique every time, yet always possesses the same timeless splendor.

If after so many years I sometimes find it difficult to recognize Chipaya, my friends, in turn, seem somewhat perplexed at the changes they see in me. It's not only my gray hair or my nearly white beard. It's that I don't question them with the same insistence they'd grown accustomed to about the ritual tables, the *mallkus,* or the mermaids.* Naturally they understand my interest in the recent transformations, but when, from time to time, we return to our long conversations on the history of the Urus,

---

*Or *serenos*. Small, long-haired creatures who live in the rivers, causing people they meet to fall sick. See Wachtel, *Le Retour des ancêtres* (see p. 141, n. 1, below), 202–3. For a description of *mallkus,* see Glossary.—Trans.

the conflicts with their Aymara neighbors, and the old customs, I sense they are reassured. I even go so far as to make a new recording of one of the stories or myths I know by heart, simply to put my friends at ease. For Martin, who has slipped into the role of my chief informant again, these are moments of quiet happiness: with a satisfied smile, he sips his tea spiked with liquor, pronouncing a vow or benediction with each swallow, and taking pleasure in the sound of his slow, deliberate voice.

§

One of the first things I am curious about are the changes that may have altered the social organization of Chipaya. During my previous visits, I witnessed what was essentially the birth and then the development of a hotly debated split in the society. Had it led to the creation of a new community?

As in the other villages of the Andean altiplano, in Chipaya the principles of the dualist order traditionally determined the distribution of land, the division of social groups, and the conception of the universe and of the sacred powers. One local particularity is that the Aransaya and Manasaya moieties are also *ayllus,* and thus form two economically separate and parallel subsections; the unity of the village is essentially expressed on the level of ritual practices and symbolic representations. In keeping with the classical model of dualist thought—the dividing up of constituent categories (high/low, masculine/feminine, etc.) and the containment of social groups one inside the other—each Chipaya moiety is composed of two sectors (Tuanchajta and Tajachajta in the Aransaya moiety, Ushata and Waruta in the Manasaya moiety, or four fourths in all), which in turn are subdivided into annexes (four in each moiety, or eight annexes in all). Administratively, the ensemble forms the canton of Chipaya, directed by a *corregidor.* Yet the main "authority" is situated within each moiety in the person of the *alcalde,* who has both civil responsibilities (collecting contributions, surveying collective works, etc.) and ritual functions (a central role in many religious holidays). It is true that since 1961 the dualist organization of Chipaya has adapted to a tripartition, with the separation, to the east of the territory, of the dunes of Ayparavi (which was declared a canton as a defense against the demands of the neighboring village of Huachacalla following a centuries-old conflict). Administratively, the new canton of Ayparavi meant that a third *ayllu* was born, functioning side by side with the two others, outside the dualist system of organization.

Inside each Chipaya moiety, each family line is

more closely associated with a particular section of the territory, where its *estancias* (hamlets) are con- centrated. Thus, on the Aransaya side, in the Ta- jachajta area to the southwest of the territory, the Camichiri section corresponds to the Guarachi family, which numbers about a dozen family heads, as well as a few Mamani allies. Its leader, Vicente, is a strong personality, a man of about fifty years old now, whose eyes shine with intelligence and sarcastic humor; his reputation as a great *yatiri* (sorcerer) has spread throughout the entire Carangas region, all the way to Chile. In 1974, when Vicente told me of his dream to transform his section into a full-fledged canton, I attributed his grandiose project to megalomania. Two years later, however, the separatist movement of Camichiri began: the inhabitants of the annex proposed establishing a new irrigation system so that they would have their own cultivated lands. They justified this project first with economic and demographic reasons: the fields prepared communally for the Aransaya moiety were no longer sufficient for the increased population. The other members of Aransaya expressed their disapproval; frequent meetings were held in an atmosphere of great tension.

The almost desertlike conditions impose special constraints on both agriculture and stock farming in

Chipaya. The high salt content of the soil necessitates the flooding of a part of the territory for more than six months in order to cultivate quinoa; the water washes the salt from the earth, and is then drained. What was a lake then becomes a cultivated field in which each family head receives a certain number of lots. But by the end of the agricultural year the soil becomes poorer as the salt returns: planting is then transferred to another area, prepared in advance by another cycle of flooding. It is thus a very intelligent system of rotation, both of the fields and of the water; the artificial lakes must succeed one another so that one field is always ready each year. While the use of the cultivated lots is individual, the irrigation and drainage are executed by collective *faenas,* which gather the men of each *ayllu* in their respective territories. The dualist organization of Chipaya is thus also manifested in a double system of irrigation: each moiety has its own offtake from the Lauca river. Despite the hydrographic complexity, there are no arms linking these two networks, which remain strictly parallel.

Two lakes shaped like elongated crescents serve as spillways for each of these two networks, at the same time providing rich pastures suitable for the aquatic farming of pigs. On either side, numerous huts with pointed roofs shelter the animals. Their outlines form a jagged horizon on the banks of the river and among the tumuli that emerges from the water, creating the effect of a miniature village: what the Chipayas call "the city of pigs." Each family head has his own herd of pigs in the lakes (as well as a herd of sheep or llamas in the *estancias*). Meanwhile, the aquatic plants on which the pigs feed also require successive cycles of irrigation and drainage, which are handled collectively. This constant circulation of water creates the close connection between the agricultural and the pastoral activities of the Aransaya and Manasaya moieties; in this way the Chipayas are still *jas-shoni*, "water men."

The double system of irrigation was in harmony with the dualist organization of Chipaya (considered within the boundaries of the canton). So the project presented in 1976 by Vicente and his partisans introduced a certain discord: they wanted to dig a new canal in order to increase the water supply of the Camichiri section, and thus organize a third system of water and land rotation. Although most of the Aransaya members were hostile to this project, they had to give in when the Guarachis, violating the rule of consensus, simply started on the work and presented the rest of the community with the fait accompli. The agreements finally reached between the members of Camichiri and of Aransaya stipulated that the fields, lakes, and pastures would henceforth be separate. This division meant both a spatial and a social reorganization for the Chipayas, who from then on were divided into four distinct groups (Camichiri, the rest of Aransaya, Manasaya, and Ayparavi). But did this new quadripartition conform to the binary logic?

The 1976 debate was all the more furious as other solutions were possible that would not have resulted in the separation of Camichiri. The other Chipaya moiety, Manasaya, although suffering from the same shortage of cultivated land, nonetheless stayed together. Along with the more explicit causes, another factor probably came into play in the separation: serious conflicts had been disturbing the village since the 1960s, when new religious groups were established—two of them Protestant (the Pentecostals and the Evangelicals), and one Catholic (the "Catechists"). The three groups, whose followers called themselves *hermanos,* or "brothers," rejected the customs considered to be idolatrous and opposed the "pagans," the term used to refer to those who continued to practice all the rituals, honoring both the saints and the *mallkus* (the Andean chthonian divinities, generally associated with the mountains). As it turns out, one of the principal leaders of the pagans hostile to the new movements

was none other than the *yatiri* Vicente, who had
many partisans in Camichiri. Until the early 1970s,
the brothers of the various sects were but a small minority and met with widespread disapproval. But
little by little, from visit to visit, I saw the number of
pagans decrease as the new religious groups gained
strength. So much so that, oddly enough, in 1982
another type of quadripartition could be observed.
The population was essentially divided into four un-
evenly distributed religious groups: the Catechists
included more than half of the Chipayas, the Evangelicals almost a quarter, the Pentecostals about a
fifth, while the pagans were but a small core of obsti-
nate rebels. This group, which now in turn met with
strong disapproval, flocked to the Camichiri annex,
which thus came to be the last refuge of the traditionalists.

I therefore had a number of questions to ask when
I returned to Chipaya seven years later: Was Vicente
able to make his dream come true, and turn his annex into a canton? Had the last pagan group held
together in the face of the seemingly invincible expansion of the new churches? In reality, the evolution of the village turned out to be more complicated
and less predictable. The Camichiri annex was still
separate yet had not been elevated to the level of a
canton, while the Aransaya moiety continued to

split apart: the three other annexes followed the example of the Guarachis, becoming autonomous with their own fields, so that the moiety still consists of four sectors at the same level (each with an auxiliary *alcalde* in charge). It is as if the logic of the dualist order had managed to compensate for the discord introduced by the separation of Camichiri, reestablishing a certain symmetry through a new type of quadripartition (all within the Aransaya moiety).

In 1984–85 the members of the other three annexes organized their own individual rotation systems for water and fields. Like the Camichiri members, they explained this redistribution by the need for expanded growing fields due to a growth in population. And the results obtained in Camichiri, at least in the beginning, seemed encouraging; all the family heads had benefited from it with a greater number of lots and more abundant harvests. But what would happen when the land became even more divided? Could four systems of rotation coexist within a single moiety of the Chipaya territory? Would the waters of the Lauca River support such an expansion of the irrigation network? The answer was not long in coming: the splitting up of Aransaya into four separate groups proved to be a disaster. The accelerated rotation of the lands caused their

deterioration, with one bad harvest after another
these past years. What is more, the lake in which
pigs were raised dried out; the animals were struck
by an epizootic disease, and the "city of pigs" is now
deserted. The Aransayas thereby lost an essential re-
source and an enormous amount of capital (more
than five hundred head of livestock). What were they
to do? I could only witness their bewilderment.
They are all the more confused as the Manasaya
members have continued to function as a community and, though not always enjoying bountiful harvests (due to variations in the climate), still have their
pigs and their livestock.

So the inhabitants of Aransaya are now thinking
of reuniting. Not by returning to the situation that
existed before the separation of Camichiri, but
rather by regrouping the four annexes two by two:
on the one side those to the west of Aransaya, on the
other those to the east. In other words, the moiety
would again be divided into two areas, Tajachajta
and Tuanchajta, a return to the way things were in
the 1930s, when cultivation of quinoa by means of
irrigation was first introduced to Chipaya. At that
time, the cultivated lands were prepared within each
quarter, and even then, after a few years, the water
problem had led to the union of Tajachajta and
Tuanchajta (in the Aransaya moiety) and of Ushata

and Waruta (in the Manasaya moiety). If the Aransayas were to resolve the problem by recombining annexes two by two, the entire ethnic group would once again be composed of four groups (Tajachajta, Tuanchajta, Manasaya, and Ayparavi), following a configuration that is both unprecedented in the history of Chipaya and more in keeping with the logic of the dualist order.

§

October is the month in which one is most likely to encounter the Chipayas in their village. For one thing, it's the sowing season: those who have gone to work elsewhere return to be assigned lots. For another, All Saints' Day is approaching, one of the most sacred moments of the year: even the migrants who have been away for a long time return to welcome the souls of the deceased, who come to visit the living for the day.

For the two weeks preceding the festival, the preparations create a certain animation in the village, as well as an increasingly perceptible tension. Sheep destined for the market in Oruro are slaughtered on patios, in front of the houses. Another new development is the incredible frequency of trucks—up to two trips to the town a week—during this time. There is only one truck in Chipaya, owned by the wealthy Mariano, but other vehicles make the round trip, one from the neighboring village of Escara, the other from Coipasa. Each departure is a major event: it takes hours to load the truck and gather the passengers; people keep coming and going, the horn is honked loudly to warn latecomers that the truck is leaving. The preparations are especially intense for those "who have a soul," that is, people who have lost a close relative within the past three years and hence must incur major expenses. What can you do when you have no animals to sacrifice? The poorest, or the most cunning, have certain tricks: they beg me to buy pieces of fabric, ceremonial slings, and never have I had so many offers to be a *compadre*!

You can't refuse godfather status, even if it's obvious that the offer is financially motivated, as when Eduardo Q. comes to see me a few days before All Saints' Day. His usual good humor suits his round, puffy face; but this time he is somber, nervous, extremely preoccupied. He comes right to the point: "I need your help because I'm expecting my mother-in-law!" I begin to smile, surprised that this visit should make him so nervous, when suddenly I realize that his wife's mother died a year ago, and that he's talking about her soul and the ritual offerings due her. Poor Eduardo! His mother-in-law terrifies him dead more than she did alive! The next day I arrive at his house at the appointed hour for the ceremony, but we are unable to proceed because his entire family is quite intoxicated. A little later, barely sober and absolutely terrified, Eduardo rushes to my house to ask for my help again: "I had a fight with my wife because of her mother. I beat her, come see, she's in terrible shape!"

Several days before All Saints' Day, Martin comes to tell me that he's been asked to participate in a ceremony which he knows is going to "interest" me. They are about to erect a tomb and renew offerings to the deceased Angela G., who was buried in a simple grave several years ago and whose soul, unable to find peace, has been tormenting her husband. When I arrive at the ceremony, at about five in the afternoon, the parents of the deceased are already at Martin's side. Martin is wearing a magnificent beige cap for the occasion. He begins by slaughtering a black sheep on top of the grave, sprinkling the blood as a drink offering toward the west (where the dead reside). Then he begins digging up earth at the site of the sacrifice, with the help of an assistant. The work advances slowly, the sun sinks on the horizon, shadows grow longer. Waist-deep into the pit, Martin probes the earth with a metal hook. "It's here!" he exclaims. He lights a cigarette so that the smoke will chase away the dangerous va-

pors, then gathers up the remains, which he lays out
bone by bone on a piece of cloth spread next to the
hole. With a mischievous little smile he announces,
"The human skeleton is composed of one hundred
and twenty-five bones!" and recites, "Cervical bone,
tibia, fibula, femur," and so on. Not only does he
pick out the bones, but he rubs them, massages
them, caresses them affectionately. Everyone grows
sentimental upon recognizing the dead woman's
tresses, perfectly preserved. The skull and bones are
carefully cleaned, her nearly intact sandals are af-
fixed, and finally Martin finds the flask of liquor
with which the body had been buried. During this
time other assistants, outside the cemetery, prepare
the mounds of earth to be used to erect the tomb.
Children appear out of nowhere, a young woman offers them candy, the colored paper wrappers fly in
the wind around the cemetery. Some fall into the
deep pit. The cloth is folded and placed with the offerings in a wooden box, which in turn is laid in the
tomb. A cross is planted just as the sun disappears
behind the mountain. To the east, the deep blue horizon turns grey, while to the west, above the Andes,
the sky grows purple. We complete the tomb in the
encroaching darkness.

As All Saints' Day approaches, the waiting becomes particularly intense: the deceased come up

more and more frequently in conversation; their souls are already gathered on the outskirts of the cemetery, waiting to visit. By noon on November 1, when the families deposit their offerings of food and drink on the tombs, you can feel a change occur: the souls are here, their presence almost palpable. The ritual has changed somewhat: in the past the bells rang continuously for more than twenty-four hours, so that the souls' visit took place against a backdrop of monotonous, repetitive music; now the bells sound only intermittently, briefly, like a call or salutation. The skulls of the founding ancestors are no longer transported to the church, but merely honored at the cemetery. The four skulls are lined up in the middle of the central row, facing south. The *alcaldes* and their wives kneel before them and pray, offering coca leaves and scattering generous offerings of alcohol. Their families form a circle around them. Cigarettes are affectionately lit for the ancestors to smoke. What a strange and intimate scene: the revered skulls with two or three burning cigarettes lodged in their nasal cavities. The cigarettes are smoked "by themselves," and this is seen as a good sign: when they burn easily to the end, the next year will be a good one, the harvest will be plentiful. When a cigarette goes out, one of the people kneeling nearby simply takes the cigarette from the

skull, puts it in his mouth, relights it, and respect-
fully replaces it in the nasal cavity.

A sense of gravity reigns that afternoon when,
back from the cemeteries, the Chipayas welcome the
souls into their homes. The offerings are laid out on
a table, a setting placed at the seat of honor: food,
drink, coca leaves, candy. The possessions of the deceased are also laid out around his or her photo
(when one is available) and a lighted candle. The
members of the family sit in a semicircle, passing
cups of liquor and remembering the deceased: stories and anecdotes are blended with tears and loud
lamentations. The family engages in conversation
with the soul, whose presence is evident, even for
me. This is when I visit my friends, before they're
totally intoxicated, to "accompany" them in their
sorrow. I feel a little awkward, sometimes, when I
didn't know the deceased very well and my con-
dolences are necessarily merely polite. And I feel
sincere sadness when I go to my friend Benito's
house, whose father, Geronimo, one of my principal
informants, died barely two months before my return to Chipaya. I recognize the photo I myself took
long ago, and which the magic of the Polaroid enabled me to give to him: here are Geronimo's features, his eyes, his silhouette; he is no longer with us
and yet he is among us today. "You see, the photo is

still here, the photo will be here forever!" Benito comments, his voice full of emotion. An identity card is also among the deceased's possessions, a detail of which sends my friend into the depths of confusion. "Look, it was valid until 1992, it's written there: why did he die before that?"

They sit with the souls all night, from the first to the second of November. It's one of the nights I worry about the most during my trips to Chipaya: the drunkards will certainly knock on my door more than once. I blow out my candles early so as not to attract them. Nevertheless, at about one in the morning I recognize Benito's voice outside my door. Under the pretext of asking for some coca leaves, he again expresses his sorrow, crying and muttering incoherently. All I can make out is, "My father taught me that . . . I owe him . . . "

On the morning of the second I return to the cemetery with the families, who accompany their souls back to their graves. The few groups who remained sober cross paths apprehensively with the howling, staggering clusters. There is the threat of a fight: in the course of coming and going to the tombs, enemies run into each other, in their drunkenness unleashing feelings of hatred. I notice a few more changes. First, outside the cemetery, in front of an improvised altar covered with a white tablecloth, the

Catechists sing a proper "mass" toward the west (the priest has left the village for the festival). Other Chipayas carry a tape player and salute the departure of the deceased to the catchy sounds of dance music. Since several players are going at the same time full blast, the farewell to the souls takes place amid a deafening cacophony. Soon the batteries wear down, the music stammers, stutters, and fades into the sound of even more heart-wrenching tears.

TWO *The Day I Was God*

I HAD SPENT YEARS FREQUENTING THE DEAD, TRY-
ing to decipher their traces in the quiet, dusty archives, in order to reconstruct the world they inhabited. Many documents from the colonial period
(the grievance of an Indian chief, the response to an
interrogation) lead one's mind to wander: one hears
the voices of the indigenous witnesses, but the sound
is muffled and fragmented, so that the impression of
spanning the distance of centuries is accompanied
by an inevitable feeling of frustration. This is essentially the way things go: the daily life we glimpse
through the archives remains fragmentary, cloudy,
by definition limited to exceptional events, while understanding them requires an analysis of the general
context in which they took place. At the same time,
the present reality of the indigenous communities
whose past I was studying also seemed distant and
fleeting to me. I was living in the comfort of cities, in
Cuzco, Potosi, or Sucre, where as far as the Indians
were concerned, one saw little else than the por-
ters who hung around hotels, or the beggars who
pressed their noses against restaurant windows.
And while I had passed through many villages in the
course of my travels, I was generally searching for
30 old papers. Like many tourists, I had visited the

floating island on Lake Titicaca, opposite Puno, where folkloric Urus exhibited their huts and rush canoes. At the time I didn't realize that my research would take a new turn when, in 1973, Jacques Ruffié asked me to contribute to the work of a team assigned to investigating the hemotypology of the populations of the Andean highlands. That is what led me to venture out of my archives into a terrain with a reputation for being difficult, into the area of a somewhat uncivilized ethnology.

What a revelation! Suddenly, traveling several centuries in the other direction, I found myself among the present-day, authentic descendants of the dead people with whom I had spent so much time in dusty archives. What was more, as Urus these living descendants found themselves marginalized and disdained by their Aymara neighbors, who considered them to be *chullpa-puchu,* rejects from the ancient dead, refuse from the first human civilization, the civilization before the sun. The Indians whose daily life I was now sharing were essentially "the defeated of the defeated," and presented a special area for research that until now I had only dreamed might exist. I became aware at the same time of the possibilities (as well as of the demands) of the intimate collaboration between history and anthropology. Subsequently, I alternated between research in the archives and field studies, the constant shifting from the living to the dead, and from the dead to the living, inevitably bringing about a slightly out-of-synch perception, both of the present and of the past.

For their part, how did the Chipayas perceive my presence? The gringos who came to this remote village fit into distinct categories: priests, pastors, or doctors. From time to time tourists would mistakenly wander into this deserted plateau, stay a few hours or a few days to take the indispensable photos, then leave after being properly fleeced. Other anthropologists, it is true, had preceded me. One or two old people could remember the distant visit of a French researcher: was it Métraux in the 1930s, or Vellard in the 1940s? The memories were extremely vague. Along with Gilles Rivière, who accompanied me on this first visit, I represented a new category: I stayed longer than an ordinary tourist and in my neophyte enthusiasm was particularly interested in the "customs," beliefs and rituals, which seemed to me highly traditional. Yet the priests and pastors preached a religion cleansed of these practices, which they considered diabolical. What was this apparently pagan gringo doing in the village?

It didn't take me long to realize that, by his very presence, the anthropologist who intrudes into a so-

cial group modifies, even perturbs, the delicate equi-
librium or disequilibrium of this group. No matter
how he behaves, he cannot control other people's interpretations of him: consciously or unconsciously
he enters into the equation among the existing fac-
tions, and while he would like to be an observer,
he may find himself manipulated instead. It is impossible to turn oneself into a purely external observer: the researcher necessarily occupies a certain
position amid the workings of the indigenous population, and finds himself assigned one role or another, which various members of the community,
based on their own agendas, attempt to make him
play. He is trapped in his own presence. Should
he proclaim himself neutral, practice ecumenism?
By the choice of his informants, the friendships he
develops, even the questions he asks, the anthropologist becomes an actor and cannot escape the in-
volvement that befalls him, despite his objections.
He can only guess at what he represents to others,
making sure to be true to himself. Is this at the price
of diplomatic maneuvers that are too subtle, of com-
promises that are too complaisant?

§

At the time of my first visit, most Chipayas called
themselves "pagans," which seemed to have no pe-

jorative connotations. For those who declared their allegiance, it meant respect for all the traditions, as well as loyalty to the beliefs of the ancestors. "It's the custom": this explanation justified rituals believed to have been practiced since time immemorial. Yet this belief was no longer universal: although in 1973 the daring innovators (Catechists, Evangelicals, Pentecostals) were in the minority, they introduced a rift in the pagan-Christian system that governed the order of religious festivals. Each year the *alcaldes* designated a certain number of *pasantes,* or "volunteers," who committed to sponsoring a saint or *mallku*'s festival the following year, on the day indicated by the calendar. These celebrations were expensive, and served to manifest the bonds of solidarity between the members of the community. To accept a *cargo,* or sponsorship, was traditionally considered an inevitable obligation as well as an honor. Which is why the brothers of the new religious movements caused a scandal when they refused to accept these customs and at the same time set a contagious example: though the system of rotating *cargos* still functioned normally, the *alcaldes* were beginning to have trouble establishing lists of *pasantes;* there were fewer and fewer volunteers. Is this why they made me an offer, the repercussions of which would permanently mark my relationship to the Chipayas?

As chance would have it, the first "authority" I met during my first visit in 1973 was none other than Santiago Condori, the pioneer of the Catechists, who then held the post of municipal agent. I dealt with him when I was looking for lodgings in the village: he immediately offered to rent me one of his huts in the Aransaya moiety, no doubt counting not only on a little extra cash but also on establishing useful relations with a gringo from such a distant country. For my part, I didn't yet know about his central role in the conflicts that were dividing the village; I would explain to informants who I hoped would collaborate that I had come to study the history of the Chipayas, which was the exact truth and explained my interest in the customs; but I was in an ambiguous situation since I was staying with Santiago, a Catechist.

At that time, the *alcalde* of Aransaya (the main authority of the *ayllu*) was Juan Quispe, a fortyish, amiable man and subtle politician, who fully endorsed my research. He may have seen this research, and the assistance he offered me, as a means to reassure the traditionalists. He himself alerted me to the fact that the best informant I could find in matters of customs would be his own father, Pablino (who was among those who thought they remembered Alfred Métraux), and his older brother, Martin, both experts in ritual practices and remarkable storytellers. My network of informants gradually grew out of this initial core to Juan's relatives and friends: his father-in-law Policarpio, officiating priest of the Kiliminti *mallku;* old Geronimo Lazaro, the officiating priest of Santiago; Geronimo's sons, Benito and Victor; and their cousin Fortunato, the sexton of the church (who therefore knew a great deal about religious festivals). Of course, from my very first visit I made a point of varying my interlocutors, and of working in the same way with members of the other *ayllu,* Manasaya. As is proper, I was also careful to alternate the location of my living quarters, one year in one moiety, the next year in the other. But I always felt most comfortable in Aransaya, no doubt because of the attachment one preserves for one's first experience in the field: I developed ties of friendship with Martin, Benito, and their parents, but also with Santiago, which over the years have proved indestructible.

One particular circumstance contributed to bind me even more closely to Aransaya. It was the surprising proposition put to me by Juan, who as *alcalde* had to establish the list of *pasantes* for the following year: Would I sponsor the festival of the Kiliminti *mallku,* one of the most important divinities of the moiety? He probably hadn't found a "volunteer" among the Chipayas, but why was he asking a

gringo who at that point was a stranger? I suppose
his offer was something of a challenge, a test: I had to show that I wasn't just an ordinary tourist passing through, that I would come back to Chipaya as I had said, and that in addition I had the means to take on lavish expenses. Perhaps Juan also wanted to strengthen the position of Aransaya over the other moiety and, as a supplementary strategy, to induce me to support the traditionalist party. What should I do? The choice seemed simple: on the one hand, if I were to refuse, I knew what a disappointment and even an offense it would be to my friends; on the other hand, if I agreed, I saw the advantages of being truly accepted by the Chipayas (or at least by a majority of them). Not to mention the prospect of having a primary role in an exciting ritual. Should it be ruled out because I would be compromising myself with the pagan group? I couldn't worry about that: it was important to show my gratitude to friends who had helped me so generously and were bestowing such an honor on me. In the end, I enthusiastically agreed to be the *pasante* of the Kiliminti *mallku*.

§

I therefore had to be back in the village, punctually, the following August 1, the day of the Kiliminti. Preparations for a stay in Chipaya were always long

and costly; I went about them feverishly, as if for a
polar expedition. They began in Paris, with routine
visits to the doctor and dentist, the purchase of pho-
tographic equipment and recording materials, and
shopping at the camping store, then continued in
several stages in Bolivia. I spent about ten days in La
Paz, at the beginning of July 1974, not only to gather
the permits necessary from the various authorities,
but also to take care of some business for the Chipayas: I knew that the previous spring the village
had experienced serious flooding, and that the entire
harvest had been lost. They therefore needed emer-
gency relief. The military authorities accepted my
request with great understanding, and promised to
send a truckload of food. The next step was the market at Oruro, a teeming world overflowing with di-
verse objects, colors, smells, as if the essence of the
high plateaus were concentrated in this one spot.
Along with my usual assorted purchases (tins of
food, kitchen utensils, bowls, candles, matches,
soap, notebooks to give as gifts to the school, cigarettes, coca leaves, etc.) I had to purchase everything
for the celebration of the festival and, in particular,
for the ceremonial meal offered by the *pasante* to the
entire village: rice, potatoes, *chuño* in astronomical
quantities, enormous packages of coca leaves, and
countless jugs of liquor. I felt a little guilty about

supporting my hosts' drinking habits, but drinking
was the custom. Nor were these expenses so easily justified to the institutions who were financing my mission.

True to my promise, I was back in Chipaya in mid-July, two weeks early, in the company of Gilles Rivière, who, like me, had agreed to return for the festival of the Kiliminti. As I wanted to live on the Manasaya side later, we avoided settling in Aransaya, and were housed in "neutral" terrain, in the office of the *corregidor* (one of the rare houses that had a brick instead of a badly packed earth floor). Our occupying, even temporarily, a house that was reserved for the highest authority of the village lent an official quality to our already unique situation. Our colleague Olivier Dollfus was supposed to join us a week later to participate in the festivities. The final step was to negotiate the purchase of a sacrificial lamb, llama, and pig (another expense to justify in the report of my mission). These were difficult negotiations, since even our friends, quite legitimately, endeavored to sell us their animals at inflated prices. We also noticed an obvious reluctance: as the days passed, the people who had agreed to sell us an animal came to tell us, one after the other, that they had to rescind their offer. Their reasons seemed unconvincing: their wife didn't want to sell it, the llama

was at an *estancia* that was too far away, the pig had
run away. The series of defections was worrisome.
Were they the result of pressures placed on the animals' owners, warnings about us? Eventually the
string of festivals that marks the end of the religious
year arrived: July 25, the festival of Santiago; July
26, the festival of Santa Ana, patron saint of the village, whose day was still celebrated enthusiastically.

The new religious year began with the day of the
mallku Kiliminti. Juan and Martin had agreed to
come for us in the early morning to take us to the
monument dedicated to the *mallku,* about fifteen ki-
lometers to the south, at the edge of the desert. Time
passed, we waited, no one appeared. Our friends
didn't arrive until nine o'clock. They were alone,
though we had planned to form a procession with
the members of Aransaya. We all waited a little
longer; no one joined us. And we still had no animals to sacrifice, as the last people had backed out.
Was this yet another test of our will? It was as if they
were creating a vacuum around us. What should we
do? Keep going. It's the day of the Kiliminti *mallku,*
we have to honor him no matter what. We set off in
our little group. In the course of our journey, we
cross over innumerable canals, vast lacustrine ex-
panses of still-frozen water. After taking off our
shoes and pants, we blithely break the layer of ice
with our bare feet and sink trembling into the cold

water and sticky mud; then, to take another step, we
have to laboriously extricate a foot, raise it, and
again break the ice from underneath. Once in a
while someone cries out; at other times laughter
punctuates our slow progress when one of us takes a
sudden slippery step.

As we advance, we are surprised to see other
Chipayas, who have come from the village, catching
up with us; little by little our group grows into a true
procession. After a few hours we catch sight of the
mallku, perched atop a slightly elevated land mass,
high and dry. Already we see dark splotches coming
and going in front of the monument: many other
groups, originating at the various *estancias,* are con-
verging at the *mallku,* arriving at the same time as
we are. A small crowd forms at the site. The spirit of
Kiliminti resides in a cone-shaped monument of
dried earth, about three feet high, with a small open
cavity facing east on top; this is the god's "mouth" in
which offerings are deposited. We immediately have
an opportunity to warm up; upon arrival we're
drawn into a bustling dance around the *mallku.* Our
Chipaya friends are calling greetings to Kiliminti,
soliciting his good will, and they encourage us to
do the same. We exchange somewhat bewildered
glances as we, in turn, twirl, stomp, and howl, conscious of how silly we look but also of the magnitude
of this sacred moment. "Long live Kiliminti! Hello

Kiliminti! Brr! Brr!" No matter how hard I try to be sincere as I dance and shout, I'm torn between embarrassment at participating in this ridiculous charade and the respect due the sacred ritual. I vacillate between these two contradictory, conflicting sentiments. What grotesque efforts I am making to be polite! But maybe this isn't so ridiculous after all. Do I really have to go through all this nonsense to be in this business? Yet aren't my Chipaya friends sincere when they cry "Hirsch! Hirsch!"?

After the initial dance in honor of Kiliminti, the main phase of the ceremony begins and, with it, a new surprise that brings us relief: as if by a miracle, three animals are present, hooves bound together, ready to be sacrificed. Policarpio, Juan's father-in-law, assumes the duties of the officiant. At the foot of the monument, assistants slaughter the llama, the lamb, and the pig; with each sacrifice, Policarpio collects the spurting blood into a cup, sprinkles it as a drink offering to the east, then sprinkles the *mallku* with it. His solemn gestures stand out against the deep blue sky, stained a sumptuous pink by the flight of enormous flocks of flamingos. Then, on a piece of cloth spread out on the ground in front of Kiliminti, Policarpio prepares the table with thirty-six small, shallow cups filled with *chicha* and ritual ingredients. He plunges his sacred stake into the ground, kneels behind it, and prays; an assistant hands him

the cups two by two and the officiant scatters their
contents in drink offerings toward the east as well. In
the meantime several women are fussing around a
wood fire: they are already preparing the meat of the
sacrificed animals. Sitting on the ground in the place
of honor, we are handed generous portions of liquor,
which we drink, paying homage with each swallow
to Kiliminti, to the other *mallku,* and to the saints;
soon we are served the most prized portions: half-
cooked tripe and internal organs. I swallow what I
can, try to offer a part of this precious gift to the
Chipaya friends around us, while one of my col-
leagues discreetly slips a handful of organs into his
pocket.

The meal continues in an atmosphere of warmth.
The *alcalde* of Aransaya, which this year happens
to be Vicente Guarachi, joins us in turn to give us
some aquatic plants. It's already early afternoon
when Olivier and Gilles remark that the wind seems
threatening and that it would be a good idea to return to the village; they leave shamelessly. Since the
pasante must preside over the ceremony until the
end, I stoically remain. The cups of liquor keep coming, my mind grows foggy, I no longer feel any embarrassment; on the contrary, I feel the affection of
my Chipaya friends all around me and am overcome
by a sense of euphoria. At least two hours pass in this
way, happily, amid greetings to the *mallku,* wishes,

and laughter. Then, almost to my regret, the moment of departure arrives. I stand, and the others
proceed to harness me up: my friends load onto my
back a basket filled with the aquatic plants offered
by the *alcalde;* I'm decked out in a long white wig
with a ponytail, and entrusted with the *mallku*'s
equally white banner. I now incarnate the god Kiliminti, who is about to visit the village.

We must arrive before the setting of the sun, so we
return at a much faster pace than we came: we dance
the whole way back, and sometimes run. Since it's
late afternoon, the ice on the lakes is entirely melted,
and the water, in contrast to this morning, feels almost warm. Now at the head of the procession, I
spin and cry "Brr! Brr!," my feet still bare yet numb
to the blades of prickly grass strewn over the pastures between the lakes. Is it drunkenness provoked
by the alcohol, the tension of the physical effort, diz-
ziness due to spinning around the countryside, or
just an illusion created by the role I'm playing? I
feel simultaneously giddy and elated; each instant
stands out intensely in slow motion; the sounds and
colors are veiled, unreal, leaving their imprint on me
with unforgettable clarity. Every time I spin around
I'm dazzled by the setting sun as it drops to the
Andes on the horizon; the blueness of the sky, until
now absolutely pure, is becoming tinted with increasingly golden reflections, while our gesticulating

shadows are growing longer. Finally we arrive at the
village: as we approach the first houses, crowds of spectators welcome us, applaud, cheer along with us. Among them are Olivier and Gilles, who were worried and have come to meet me. They later told me how surprised they were to see this dancing troop appear: they didn't recognize the leader of the procession, waving a white flag. I was somehow transfigured.

The moments of grace one experiences as a god inevitably come to an end once one falls back into the ordinary human world. The party is now over: we head toward the church to salute Santa Ana from the doorstep, in the semidarkness of the approaching night. Unharnessed, I sit down on the steps and barely have the time to put a shoe back on when an announcement is made: "They're coming from Manasaya!" There is fear a scuffle might break out; I follow, limping, as Gilles and Olivier quickly drag me toward the house. Finally back to earth, I return to the prosaic objects of our encampment, lit by the slim candlelight, while my attentive friends prepare a good hot soup.

§

For a long time I thought I'd made a mistake by accepting the sponsorship of Kiliminti. Then I changed my mind. My 1974 stay in the village, one

of my longest (almost five months), was certainly
very difficult. After Gilles and Olivier left, the day after the festival, I remained alone with my Chipaya
friends and moved into a Manasaya hut rented to me
by my *compadre* Pedro, one of the leaders of the traditionalist party of the "other side." He's someone I
never really got along with: a quarrelsome alcoholic,
he had mastered the art of transforming the slightest
incidents into major scandals. Since he too claimed
to be a *yatiri,* he spent his time pulling cards from a
deck, and forced me into interminable divination
sessions; at first I was interested in these, but ended
up despising them. I became superstitious myself,
and was afraid he would announce some catastrophe! But Pedro was also a good informant, with
whom I was able to deepen my inquiry into the par-
ticularities of Manasaya. Nevertheless our conversations followed an unchanging, and frustrating,
course, for he regularly reached for his pocket flask
to fill his cup. Initially clear and precise, his explanations became increasingly confused and inarticulate
as the interview progressed.

The difficulties I experienced in 1974 resulted
from a variety of causes. While my moving to Manasaya after the festival of Kiliminti manifested my
good will toward its people, it didn't automatically
erase the grudge they held against me for having fa-

vored Aransaya first. They in turn asked me when I would sponsor a festival in their moiety. And since there was no way I could return to the village the following year, nor assemble the necessary sum, I was forced to evade the question. It was a delicate and complex situation, the more so since the Pentecostals and the Evangelicals—two groups that were rapidly growing—were intrigued, even shocked, by my friendship with the pagans. And each side's animosity was brought to the surface because of a serious mistake I had made at the beginning of my stay. Naively, I had thought I could announce the imminent arrival of the provisions truck that the military authorities had promised to send to Chipaya, which was supposed to leave La Paz at the end of July. Weeks and months passed, August, September, October had come and gone, still no truck appeared. The Chipayas' questioning became more and more urgent. Soon they started reproaching me, accusing me: I had fooled them, tricked them with false promises, I was a liar! No matter how sincerely I protested, I couldn't escape the fact that the truck still hadn't come. What could I do? Whenever I heard the sound of a motor (which was rare), I hurriedly scanned the horizon. Each time I was disappointed. This obsessive waiting took on quasi-messianic overtones. My Aransaya friends believed in me and took up my defense. For weeks I found myself at the center of debates: my presence heightened the village's internal dissension.

The end of my stay was approaching; I was beginning to feel desperate. My credibility, my honor, were at stake. "If I leave under these conditions," I told myself, "it'll be a total failure, I'll never be able to come back." Then suddenly, a week before the date set for my departure, a miracle occurred. Again the sound of a motor, headlights in the darkness, I begin to run: yes, it's the truck! There's great emotion in the village, it's all very theatrical: I am instantly transformed, from shame to triumph. A big celebration is organized before my departure, everyone dances, it's a mass reconciliation. My worst detractors confuse me by going down on their knees to ask my forgiveness: I in turn have to reassure them. It all turned out to be a matter of bureaucracy: the truck arrived four months late because certain forms had to be filled out, certain signatures had to be obtained, the rules had to be respected!

My reconciliation with the brothers of the various sects was sealed during subsequent visits in 1976 and 1978, when I greatly expanded my inquiry to include the religious movements that were transforming Chipaya society. This was the moment when their spectacular progress was to lead to a reversal of the balance of power, to the marginalization of the pagan group. Working with the brothers wasn't always easy. I explained to them that, as a student of the history of Chipaya, I was interested in the history of their church because their church was an integral part of this history. But they couldn't help but interpret my inquiry as a first effect of divine grace. Though I was very honest in explaining to them that I wasn't a member of their church and had no intention of converting, they were nonetheless convinced that I would wind up worshiping in their faith. Thus an inevitable ambiguity took root: during the church services I was obliged to attend, I felt uneasy at the undeserved consideration and friendliness shown me. The discrepancy between my interest in these brothers and their expectations of me made me worry I might seem to be tricking them again. At the same time, my pagan friends might wonder, with apparent reason, about my attitude: Weren't they being betrayed by the former *pasante* of Kiliminti? Fortunately, many of them in turn adopted the faith of the new churches, so that I was basically just following the flow.

Furthering my integration into the village, while accentuating the uniqueness of my position, were the journeys on which I invited my friends Martin, Benito, and Fortunato to join me, first in 1974, then

in 1976, to visit the other surviving Urus, the Moratos of Lake Poopo and the Iru-Itus of Desaguadero. Elsewhere I have told of the moving encounter
between these descendants of humanity before the
sun, all *chullpa-puchu,* who until then had only
heard about each other, but had never met.[3] It's true
that the impact of this experience primarily concerned a few of my oldest friends, but they immediately shared their discovery with the other inhabitants of the village upon their return. My role as
mediator between the different groups of the Uru
"nation" added something of an ecumenical dimension to my presence. In addition, over the years I had
been able to acquire a certain knowledge of Uru history myself: the documents I had assembled at the
archives of Corquemarca, Poopo, and Sucre, which I
had annotated with my collaborators, revealed unsuspected aspects of the Uru past. The Chipayas
would consult me on this topic, so that, paradoxically, I in turn became an informant to them! Martin,
in particular, loved to ask me questions: we would
converse in a learned fashion, like members of an ac-
ademic society, exchanging our interpretations, our
doubts and hypotheses. Time, in short, had done its
work, and I think I can say that a wide group of
adults of all beliefs finally saw me for what I was: a
historian of Chipaya society.

Still, something remained of the day I had been god. According to custom, former *pasantes* are honored by being given the name of the festival they sponsored. So the Chipayas often called me "Kiliminti" (until my last visit, fifteen years later), in an affectionately humorous tone. At first I was annoyed to be repeatedly reminded of such an old episode, but then I accepted the inevitable; after all, it was a sign of a kind of Chipaya citizenship. I kept the nickname as a souvenir of those moments of grace I lived so long ago.

THREE

The Midnight Confession

THOUGH MY RETURN TO CHIPAYA WAS PRIMARILY A friendly visit, I had an ulterior motive. There had been a serious disruption in the village in 1978, which I'd heard about through rumors and certain articles that appeared in the regional newspaper (*La Patria* of Oruro). A charge of causing "a threat to the public health" had been made, a military detachment had been dispatched, and several Chipayas had been arrested, then imprisoned in Oruro. My attempts to learn more about the matter during my previous visit in 1982 had met with no success. The slightest allusion to the affair made people uncomfortable, and even my best friends were reticent and preferred not to talk about it: the subject was taboo. The main protagonists (the ones that weren't in prison) had never returned to the village, so I couldn't question them; for this reason my previous visit had left me with a feeling of frustration that I was finally hoping to dispel. What had happened?

The affair involved *kharisiri,* one of the greatest dreads of the Andean world. The *kharisiris* (also called *lik'ichiris* or, in Peru, *nakaq,* or *pishtakos*) are more or less mythical characters who accost their victims on deserted roads or break into their houses at night, sending them into a deep sleep by use of

52

various powders, and taking advantage of their unconscious state to extract their fat (or their blood
according to other, more recent versions). Several
days later the victims feel weak, suffer from a kind
of apathy, or anemia, then die. In the ethnographic
literature (to which we shall return), the *kharisiri*
generally appears with the features of a gringo, the
diabolical incarnation of the outside world. A number of foreigners who have worked locally—doctors, engineers, even anthropologists—and who
considered themselves well integrated into their
communities have had the alarming misfortune of
being suspected of these criminal actions: they had
no choice but to flee as quickly as possible.

It is easy to see why investigations into matters of
this kind are anything but simple. What intrigued
me particularly, in the Chipaya case, was that the accused parties were neither from the gringo world
nor from another village but belonged to the indigenous group itself. I knew that similar cases had occurred in the region, contradicting the classical
interpretation of the phenomenon. In Orinoca, near
Lake Poopo, a village resident was accused of the
same crime in 1983. Since this type of offense is not
recognized by the Bolivian justice system, the community assembly sets up its own tribunal; in this
case the unfortunate party was burned alive, his

ashes scattered to the wind. When the regular judges
attempted to intervene, seeking those who had insti-
gated the punishment, they encountered a wall of
silence—an admission, at the same time, of collective complicity. Could a similar drama have taken
place in Chipaya, where I had so many *compadres*
and so many friends?

§

Ten years had passed since the affair. When I cautiously raised the subject of *kharisiris,* I again found
my interlocutors somewhat uncomfortable, though
slightly more talkative than before. According to
them, in 1978 many Chipayas had been stricken
with a strange illness, characterized by a sudden fa-
tigue, a state of prostration from which many died.
Suspicious-looking spots were found on the bod-
ies of the sick (on their arms and chests), little dots
that seemed to have been caused by the pricks of a
needle: these traces clearly demonstrated that they
had been victims of a *kharisiri.* Upon checking the
official records for that year, I found no more deaths
than for the previous or following years. Instead, I
found fewer. In 1976 there were 12 deaths; in 1977,
16; in 1978, 7; in 1979, 7; in 1980, 10; and in 1981,
9. It is in 1977, then, that we observe a rise in mor-
tality: Was this simply a delay in their awareness of

the demographic situation? Other factors certainly come into play. In the meantime, my investigation was going nowhere, and would have remained cursory if, once again, I had not benefited from exceptional circumstances.

I had been in the village for one week when, among a group of workers gathered near Aransaya to build a house (a "canteen," the construction of which had been initiated by the priest), I recognized Gregorio, the principal party accused in the *kharisiri* affair. Cynically, I rejoiced in the idea that his presence might allow me to further my inquiry, and I began keeping an eye out for him. Seeing him arrive one day by bicycle, I managed to bump into him at a curve in the path. In response to my friendly greeting, he stopped, gave me a big-toothed smile, yet spoke caustically, almost aggressively: "You're back? After all these years you haven't forgotten us? Are you going to make a sacrifice at Kiliminti?" I was silly enough to answer: "You know that Kiliminti doesn't exist anymore! That's all in the past."

Gregorio, now about forty-five years old, a member of the Manasaya moiety, had been a good informant during my first visits: I appreciated his clear and detailed explanations, but little by little, finding his insatiable desire for gifts decidedly too self-interested, I had stopped working with him. No doubt he had been angry with me (Was he still angry with me?) for moving on to other interlocutors, who had become my friends. Which is why I didn't hesitate to suggest a renewal of our former collaboration. This time he was the evasive one. A subtle game began in which he would come closer, then duck away; lure me in, then avoid me. At times Gregorio would promise to come see me, and I'd wait for him in vain; at other times I would go to his house at the appointed hour, and no one would be there. For another two weeks, no matter how cleverly I maneuvered, we missed one appointment after the next. I had the impression that he wanted to talk to me but couldn't make up his mind to do so. More frustrated than ever, I resigned myself to not seeing him, when, on the next-to-last Sunday in October, Gregorio arrived unexpectedly at my house: he proposed to sell me an *ira*.[4] I was constantly receiving offers of this kind and refused them as often as I could, but this time I accepted at once, even at the inflated price he was asking. "Come get it tonight," he said, "I'll prepare it for you." Nevertheless, I was hardly surprised when, that night, I again found his door closed.

The next morning, Monday, October 23, at the crack of dawn, I am barely awake when I hear a knock: it's Gregorio coming to apologize: "I had to go to my *estancia* to care for the flock. I didn't get the *ira* ready because my wife is against it, she doesn't want me to sell it. But tonight I'll come to your house, I have some things to tell you!" He announces this visit with unusual conviction, his voice a bit shaky but full of resolution, his gaze firm: I sense that something important is happening. As if to make less of it and to encourage him, I tell him that other informants have told me the stories of their lives, and that I would like to get his story. He seems determined, but will he change his mind? I spend the day in feverish expectation, not even chatting with my usual visitors; I cut conversations short and wander around the village instead, then meticulously prepare the cassettes and tape recorder. I even inform my friends that I won't be free that evening, so as to avoid untimely interruptions. Will he come?

Night has long fallen when Gregorio finally arrives. He carries coca leaves and cigarettes, as usual, but he isn't at ease; on the contrary, he wriggles, agitated, casting worried glances about him. The man before me is visibly terrified. He starts to tell the story of his life, but soon his tale is overrun by the drama that has destroyed him. And gradually as he speaks, I myself am filled with horror.

§

Brother, here it is. Since childhood, I have lived as an orphan, with no mother and no father. My

The Midnight
Confession

grandfather raised me, since my mother had entrusted me to him. I suffered, my grandfather sent me to work for other people, for the others, the Aymaras; I would go off crying, alone, I would watch the llamas in the mountains. My grandfather also stayed alone, his wife died, and soon he died too. I had a brother, a younger brother, but he had stayed with my mother. But I was always an orphan. When my grandfather died I was seventeen, I was very poor, I had nothing, no house, no money, no flock, nothing, nothing.

I married very young. My father-in-law had no sons, he took me in but I suffered a great deal. I was ignorant, I didn't know what it was to live as husband and wife. My wife wanted to order me around, she had her father and her mother with her, and I had no one on my side. I fought with my father-in-law, I was very unhappy. Then I thought of going to work in Chile. There I worked four months and managed to save enough money to buy a bicycle. At that time there were almost no bicycles here. When I came back, my wife and father-in-law were very kind to me. Then I left the village again, I returned to Chile, I continued to save. Each year I went back there for two months, three months. I bought coca, liquor, and I traded them: first for one lamb, then for others. My flock grew, multiplied. I already thought

I was somebody, I built a house, bought utensils for my home. So by going to work each year I saved, I began to have things, a small business, I set up a shop in my house, and I was elected to an official post, I was a community official.

First I was responsible for the organization of peasant workers, and so, with my own money, for the community, I bought a typewriter. Then, as president of the School Auxiliary Council, I took the necessary steps with the administration, traveled all the way to La Paz, obtained twenty benches, and inaugurated the new education unit. After that, they elected me to alcalde *of Manasaya. That was in 1977. I worked for the village, built a house with a metal roof to serve as a collective warehouse. Then, all of the northern sector of Manasaya wanted to become independent, just as it happened in Aransaya. But I kept the community together, I made them sign an act, the papers are registered, so that we would continue to live together. As* alcalde, *I worked a great deal, and undertook many of the expenses.*

It was the following year, in 1978, on All Saints' Day, that I was persecuted. Here's how it happened. There was a young man, a liar, Luciano F., who publicly bragged, maybe because he was drunk: "I know how to do kharisiri, *I know how to extract*

*blood!" He told this to people, on All Saints' Day.
So they arrested him, beat him to make him talk: "It
can't be that you are alone, others work with you,
tell us who!" At first Luciano didn't want to admit
anything: "No, I was just kidding." They threatened him, beat him some more, and he gave the
names of two other youths from Ayparavi. They arrested them too, everyone was saying: "All these
sick people, these scars, it must be true." But for all
that, there was no proof, it was all rumor, slander.
The next day, Friday the 3d, they called a tribunal
for that evening. I suspected nothing: that day, inno-
cently, I had baked some bread to sell. Then I went
to the tribunal.*

*Everyone was assembled. They questioned the
two youths from Ayparavi: "What did you do it
with?" "With a little machine" (una maquinita).
"And where is that instrument now?" Then one of
them gave my name: "We gave the machine back to
Gregorio M., he owns it." They sold me off like that,
casting the blame on me. But in all conscience,
brother, there was nothing to this, I had never done
anyone harm in my life.*

"But why you," I asked, "why did they give your
name?"

That I don't know. Envy, jealousy. Because I live
well, without problems with my wife. Because I had
a little money, a little business, because things were
going well for me, everything was going well.

So they arrested me too, beat me with their fists,
with their feet, tortured me: "Talk, where is the ma-
chine? They say it's at your house, confess!" But
what could I admit? Even if I told lies, there was no
machine at my house, nothing. All I could do was
suffer, be martyred like Christ. For three days and
two nights I was martyred. The three communities
gathered together, Aransaya, Manasaya, and
Ayparavi: one great tribunal, all these people, a
crowd.

They blindfolded me, dragged me naked to the
square, tied me to a cord like a llama. Then they
hung me in the tribunal, bound hand and foot, up-
side down, from my feet, and they beat me to make
me confess: "Speak, speak! Where is the machine?"
They whipped me, blood was pouring from my
nose, from my mouth, they collected my blood in a
basin. I lost consciousness, I don't remember any-
more. But I didn't speak, I don't think so. If I did
speak, I told lies, I was being tortured, I don't re-
member. I was completely innocent, brother, inno-
cent, it was all lies.

Then they took me to a house at the edge of the

village, near Aransaya. I couldn't walk anymore, my entire body was covered with wounds, sores, I was bleeding all over. They locked me in there, I remained unconscious, with nothing to drink, nothing to eat, until Sunday, I was almost dead. They had tortured me the way Christ was tortured. They wanted to kill me, and they certainly would have killed me if I hadn't been saved by the regiment from Huachacalla.

My brother Hermogenes and my brother-in-law Maximo, seeing that I was being tortured, that they were going to assassinate me, took their bicycles and went to Huachacalla, to the barracks, to warn the regiment. My brother returned Saturday afternoon, saying: "A military detachment is coming!" But they arrested my brother too, and tortured him like me. It wasn't until Sunday, at about noon, that Maximo arrived with the regiment. The officers asked for me: "Where is he?" When they saw me, all bloody, they said: "Poor thing! What's going on here?" The commander wanted to send me to the hospital in Huachacalla, but the people of the community, of three communities, were against it: "No, no! This kharisiri, we have to kill him!" They took the four of us who were accused to Sabaya, threw us in prison, and I was further mistreated. The people of Chipaya wanted to have me executed, but the subprefect told them that they couldn't do it without a trial: "We must punish according to the law." So they sent me to Oruro, to the prison in Oruro. I was sick, almost dead, but they didn't put me in the hospital. I cried every day, I wanted to leave this world myself: for them to kill me off, but I was heartbroken when I thought of my children.

While I was in prison, at Oruro, the people of Chipaya continued to persecute my family, they threatened my brother Hermogenes, my brother-in-law Maximo; even my wife, who was pregnant, they tortured her too, and they showered her with lies: "Your husband talked, he said you know where the machine is, now tell us!" They wouldn't let her go out, she was a prisoner. My daughter who was twelve years old came all by herself to Oruro, dressed in her aqsu,[5] to warn me in my prison cell: "They want to kill Mama!" My youngest children, two boys, four and five years old, were also threatened, beaten, so mistreated that they've remained half-idiots, simpleminded, and they can't learn in school anymore.

Everything I had I lost: members of the community took everything, they emptied my house, my shop, they divided up all my merchandise, everything was stolen, I had nothing left. I had two hundred sheep, pigs, I lost everything, even my bicycle.

The Chipaya authorities, the alcaldes, Honorio L. and Felipe P., accompanied by about twenty *people, came to Oruro. They began making accusations, published lies in* La Patria. *A trial was held. Doctors, professors, and lawyers discussed the affair: they all said that it wasn't possible, that such a thing doesn't exist, that it's a belief with no foundation, a legend. The Catechist brothers defended me, and the bishop of Oruro also helped me. The presiding judge decided to free me, the law was in my favor, I was innocent of all charges. And he threatened the people of Chipaya: "Ignorant peasants, savages, how could you treat an honest person like this? You're the ones who should be punished!"*

I stayed in prison one month. They let me go, but I obtained no compensation, neither for the insults, nor for the things that had been stolen from me, nor for my injuries, the blood that had been spilled, nothing. Since there was no way I could go back to Chipaya, I went to Huachacalla, I lived there alone for several months, separated from my family, who continued to be persecuted. It was only seven months later that father Gilberto was able to go to the village in a jeep and bring my wife back, rescue her, with the children. A furious crowd gathered at the square to threaten them, and it wasn't easy to get them into the car and get away.

I was already a Catechist follower; it was then, in Huachacalla, that I took a course to become a Catechist brother as well. I began working again, going to Chile to start saving again. But I couldn't work as before because of my injuries, I'm handicapped, weak, uncoordinated. Several years later, I returned to Chipaya, but they still mistreat me, I'm still persecuted. My children are also persecuted at school, the other students look down on them and insult them: "The kharisiri's *children!" I can't stay here any longer. Brother, what should I do?*

So Gregorio appeared to have come to me in search of commiseration, of sympathy. I knew that Chipaya, which seemed so peaceful, was home to interminable conflicts and fierce hatred, but I was horrified to hear the names of some of my *compadres* and friends included among the culprits in this affair. How could I help but feel ashamed, at the same time, after all my clever maneuvering to get him to talk? I listen with fascination to the story I had wanted to hear for so long, but have I the right to take advantage of the distress of a man at the end of his rope, like a vampire myself, in order to study a scientific object—the phenomenon of *kharisiri?* For I did have the professional reflex to press the record button, and to tape Gregorio's confession. The rest of his story is equally poignant.

They never stop slandering me, I'm not safe, my life is being threatened. Because now, it's starting all over again. Some people have gotten sick, and they're all saying: "It's the kharisiri again, it must be him, the sick have needle marks, scars, it's the kharisiri!" The other day, the alcalde of Manasaya, Cornelio, called a meeting to alert the members of the community: "Be careful! It's back again: my wife is sick, there are needle marks. Be on the look-out, there may be foreigners, suspicious people wandering around the village at night." I realized I was in danger again, I told them: "Our body is but misery, dirt, we may have many scars, they don't necessarily come from what you think. In the past I was slandered, persecuted, but I'm not afraid: I'm ready to sacrifice my body, like Christ." "We're not thinking of you," they responded. But I'm sure they suspect me, they think I'm guilty, that I'm the kharisiri.

"So some people are sick at the moment?" I asked (since I hadn't noticed any). "Since when?"

For the past few weeks. I'm afraid they're going to arrest me, that they're going to make a martyr of me again, persecute my family. And this time they'll kill me. Yet there is no evil in my heart, I've been chosen in this world, like Christ. I know that at the moment they're spying on me, they're watching me. Brother, what should I do? Should I stay in the village or go to the city? Brother, can you help me?

This is a cry of distress, a call for help. Gregorio's hands are shaking, his forehead is bathed in sweat, even I feel dizzy: not only is he telling me the story of his experience, but now I'm involved! How can I not help him? A terrible thought also creeps into my head, a dreadful doubt: Can I trust him? What if someone were to see us, conversing mysteriously in the dark of night? To all evidence, I'm an accomplice. Worse still, I suspect a Machiavellian plan: Why did Gregorio finally tell me his whole story if not to compromise me in turn? Knowing that he's being watched, is he trying to designate me as the real "boss" by coming to my house, to cast the blame on me, just as the youth of Ayparavi did to him? Will he pretend to have passed the infamous "machine" on to me? And if there really is a *kharisiri* affair right now in the village, I'll have no choice but to make a fast getaway! When Gregorio finally leaves, late into the night, pleading for my help (and promising to bring me all the documents in his possession the next day), I am surprised to find myself carefully barricading the door behind him.

§

After reexamining Gregorio's fears, and my own, for the rest of the night, it strikes me that a hasty departure is out of the question: it would be an admission of some sort of guilt. Nevertheless, when Martin comes to visit me the next morning, I ask him with particular interest, in what I hope is an innocent manner, after the health of this person and that. No, no one is sick, everything seems calm, at least on the Aransaya side. But in the other *ayllu*? I head to Cornelio's, the *alcalde* of Manasaya, with whom I recently established a relationship of *compadrazgo*. In response to my concern, he tells me that my *compadre* feels a little "tired." That's all he says. I seem to detect some hesitation in his attitude, a fleeting glance. Am I imagining things? He makes no reference to the meeting of community members that Gregorio mentioned, and I am careful not to bring it up.

I am wandering, perplexed, through the village alleyways when, in the afternoon, still in Manasaya, I come across an unusual scene: Celestino G., in the middle of his patio, is bending barechested over a basin, washing himself. He is one of the prominent members of the Pentecostal group, someone I often converse with. I have always known him to be sickly, and, in fact, since the beginning of my visit he has been complaining of mysterious pains. Celestino is also one of those named by Gregorio as among the most unrelenting accusers. When I get closer, I say hello without interrupting him. There is something disturbing about this spectacle, for aside from de-fleaing sessions one virtually never sees Chipayas attending to their personal hygiene. Celestino is conscientiously rubbing his arms and chest, and scrutinizing his skin. I realize right away that he is searching for suspicious marks, possible traces of the *kharisiri!*

That evening I have a long session with Martin. My friendship for him has not been betrayed: I know he wasn't one of Gregorio's persecutors. Since yesterday the tension has been unbearable. This time I approach the subject head on, revealing to him that the unfortunate party has come to ask for my help: Does he really think he's guilty? Martin remains cautious: "God only knows!" He remembers that in 1978 he himself fell ill: one morning, he discovered needle marks in his left arm; the following few days he was weak, exceedingly tired. So he thinks he was a victim of a *kharisiri* but grants that, as far as Gregorio is concerned, "they found no proof." On the other hand, Martin adds, in Orinoca the "proof" was discovered: a kind of syringe connected by a tube to a small machine ("a box that looks like your tape recorder!"). As for the current situation in the village, he confirms that while things are calm in Aransaya, there is some trouble in Manasaya. And Martin concludes: "Gregorio should

watch out on All Saints' Day, something could happen to him!"

The approach of the holiday certainly contributes
to the general tension: it was the day after All Saints'
Day that the 1978 crises broke out, and an anni-
versary of this kind no doubt rekindles Gregorio's
anxiety, as well as a certain collective fear in Manasaya. The next days will be critical. Impatiently, I
await the friends who are supposed to pick me up
after the holidays and take me back in the van. Does
this strange climate make people more talkative?
Pieces of information about the affair abound, the
picture fills in. During this time one vaudevillesque
episode follows another, as I find myself surrep-
titiously visiting interlocutors (often my *compadres*)
who are themselves mortal enemies with one another. Upon entering or leaving one of their homes, I
cautiously glance both ways, taking care to follow
complicated detours between neighboring homes,
smiling at them all in a curious mixture of sincerity
and hypocrisy. Inadvertently, a couple of these enemies encounter one another at my own house, which
makes everyone uncomfortable; since it would be
rude to leave precipitously, they stand there, side by
side, hanging their heads, surrounded by a weighty
silence that I persistently try to break by talking
about the rain or the wind.

On October 31, Gregorio prudently leaves the village and stays in Huachacalla for the duration of the holiday. He is wise to do this, for the drunks are more numerous than I had imagined, and the danger all the greater. I have promised to take him back to Oruro with me in the van, to find him a safe place to stay and to introduce him to friends who might be able to find him a job in town. The day of my departure, when he climbs into the van, my support becomes public, surprising many Chipayas. At the risk of compromising myself definitively in their eyes (of being burned, at least metaphorically), I leave in the company of the *kharisiri*.

FOUR

Tales of Vampires

THE *KHARISIRI* PRESENTS TRAITS THAT ARE BOTH
constant and manifold in space and in time, mani-
festing his capacity for adaptation to a wide range of
contexts. The series of terms used to designate him,
varying regionally, forms a coherent semantic core.
Nakaq comes from the verb *nakay:* "to slaughter";
pishtako from *pishtay:* "to cut into pieces, to slaughter"; *kharisiri* from *kharina:* "to cut something with
a sharp instrument (a knife or a razor)"; while *lik'i*
means "tallow" or "animal fat.⁶" Etymologically,
then, we are talking about a "slaughterer" who spe-
cializes in "extracting fat" from the human body; a
relationship, even an equivalence, is thereby fundamentally established between fat and blood.

Further, this relationship seems implied, in the
Andean tradition, by the name of the god Viracocha,
to whom the original myth attributes the creation
and order of the world. The association of the terms
wira and *qocha* (in Quechua), or *wila* and *qota* (in
Aymara), can be translated, literally, as "sea of fat"
or "lake of blood." If we look at their derivatives,
the terms have connotations that lead to notions
such as "reserve of vital fluids" or "creation principle."⁷ In the Andean world, indeed, blood and
fat are among the essential offerings to the sacred

powers: the sacrifice of slaughtered animals and the offering of their blood constitute the opening sequence of all religious ceremonies. Animal fat (generally llama fat) is one of the basic ingredients in the composition of ritual tables *(mesas)*.[8] These offerings, which by definition are voluntary, suggest reciprocity and are inscribed in a system of interconnected relationships: men benefit from the protection accorded by the saints or the *mallkus* in exchange for what they give. Inversely, the *kharisiri* makes any sort of reciprocity impossible, since his victim is human and he steals his vital fluids.

In the ethnographic literature, the *kharisiri* is described as a white man or a mestizo with a ragged look: ruddy complexion, piercing eyes, unkempt hair, and a shaggy beard. Sometimes he wears ordinary clothes, sometimes a sackcloth tunic cinched at the waist by a sword belt into which he slips a long pig-sticker with a sharpened blade. Slung over his shoulder he carries another terrifying weapon, a lasso made from human leather. Yet the *kharisiri* is of this world, a human being, even though he possesses magical powers and acts just like the "condemned" of the other world, who wander among us searching for innocent souls to devour. Indeed, this slaughterer travels the wilderness of the high planes on the lookout for innocent travelers, attacking them at dusk or at night, near bridges or at the bend of deserted paths. With the help of a blowpipe, he sprays his victim with a powder made of ground human bones, throwing him into a deep sleep. Then the *kharisiri* extracts his fat, which is used either for founding church bells or for concocting medical remedies. The victims either disappear (having been buried under the bridge or completely devoured), or wake up, continue their journey, then die of anemia a few days later.[9]

§

Understandably, thanks to the nature of the written sources, the *nakaq* or *kharisiri* figure is rarely mentioned in historical documents. It is all the more remarkable, then, that the theme appears, clearly identifiable, as early as the second half of the sixteenth century: the chronicler Cristobal de Molina speaks of the fear that spread among the Indians of the central Andes in 1571. A rumor was circulating that the Spanish had come to Peru in search of human fat, which they used to cure certain illnesses. The terrified Indians avoided all contact with the white men, refused to serve them, and went into hiding. They dared not enter the homes of the Spanish for fear of being killed, once inside, for their fat.[10] Cristobal de Molina attributes this rumor, which was intended to "spread hatred between the Indians and the Spanish," to the preachers sent by Titu Cusi—the Inca rebel from Vilcabamba who resisted the expeditions against him until 1572. The chronicler also establishes a link between Titu Cusi and the Taqui Ongo millenarist movement, which, beginning in 1565, brought about the revolt of part of the Indian masses of central Peru. That the relationship between the Inca of Vilcambamba and the *Taqui Ongo* is still in question, despite Cristobal de Molina's affirmation, is irrelevant here: what is important is that the theme of the *kharisiri,* assimilated into Spanish, appears for the first time, historically, in the context of a profound crisis in the indigenous society and a movement to reject colonial domination.

The *Taqui Ongo* preachers travel from village to village, exhorting the Indians to restore the *huacas* (the indigenous deities) destroyed by the Christians. They claim that ever since the Spanish conquest these divinities are no longer receiving the ritual sacrifices, that they are wandering about abandoned, "dying of thirst and hunger."[11] In revenge, they send sickness and death to all Indians who agree to be baptized.[12] On the other hand, those who reject Spanish domination but do penance and return to the cult of the *huacas* will be saved. The preachers restore life to the former deities with "resurrection" rituals, bringing offerings of *chicha* and corn to the ruins of the sacred sites. Already the *huacas* have manifested their return in spectacular fashion by becoming incarnate in their followers: "possessed," they enter into a state of ecstasy, lose consciousness, sing, dance in circles, and become objects of veneration themselves.[13] What is more, now that they have been revived, the *huacas* are preparing to wage a new battle against the Christian god, who will be vanquished in turn. "The Spanish will be killed, their cities swallowed up, and the sea will swell and drown them, abolishing their memory."[14] The Christian god is at the end of his *mita,* his "tour of command," and "the *huacas* will recreate another world and other men."[15] The Taqui Ongo prophets are announcing nothing less than a flood, a cosmic event: the end of a world and the promise of a new era. This is clearly a millenarist-type movement, developed in response to the breakdown of structure experienced by the indigenous society following the European invasion.

What is meant by Taqui Ongo, the name of this movement? The expression means literally "singing sickness," or "dancing sickness": the term *taki* applies to all sorts of "song," sacred or profane, accompanied by dance or not, whereas the term *ongoy,* which designates "sickness," is also associated with

the constellation of the Pleiades, the observation of
which, according to Andean tradition, allows us to predict meteorological phenomena, calamities, and epidemics.[16] In one part of his chronicle, Guaman Poma de Ayala lists a series of illnesses, including Taqui Ongoy, which the sorcerers healed by extracting the source of the illness from the body using suction.[17] Is it a kind of trance dance which, in the case of the millenarist movement, is provoked by the *huacas* who possess their worshipers? Further research tells us that the Taqui Ongo penitence ritual is reminiscent of the one practiced in Cuzco at the time of the Incas, during the Situa festival, which was celebrated to expel sickness. We might also wonder whether the Taqui Ongo bears some relation to the waves of epidemics (smallpox, the plague) that spread throughout the Andean world following the European invasion, bringing a demographic catastrophe to the indigenous population. Indeed, from their point of view, how can these new illnesses, and such a death rate, be explained? Two contrary but not mutually exclusive causes are possible: on the one hand, as we saw, the abandoned *huacas* are punishing the Indians (and their cult must be restored); on the other hand, the Spanish are involuntarily the cause of the epidemics. Is it any wonder, then, that the theme of the *nakaq*, identified with the white man, should appear in this context? The opposite of

the healing sorcerer, since he extracts the vital substance from the Indians, he merely transfers the tragic reality into a thinly disguised metaphoric form.

The theme of the sorcerer who heals through suction can, of course, be reversed and transformed into the sorcerer who kills by draining his victim's blood: this is the case of the *cauchus* or the *runapmicuc*, described by Arriaga in his treatise on "the extirpation of idolatry in Peru" (written in 1621), who "gain access into homes by sprinkling powder made of human bones" in order to plunge the inhabitants into a deep sleep.[18] But this purely indigenous character seems to derive from a different semantic grouping: he may be one of the components of the *nakaq* cluster, without incorporating the element that makes the latter original, that is, his association with the Spanish. More than a century after the Taqui Ongo, this association returns with charges against the Bethlehemites, who settled in Cuzco in 1690 and founded a hospital in 1700. Father Joseph García de la Concepción, author of a history of the order published in 1723, tells of "certain bad treatments inflicted on the friars, resulting in exemplary punishments:[19]

> The affair consisted in making these boors believe that the Bethlehemites were men sent to this country by the King to slaughter the

Indians and extract their fat, in order to pro-
cure this remedy for the dispensary of His
Majesty . . . Full of fear, the Indians ensured
their safety by avoiding the friars, whom
they considered to be cruel, life-threatening
enemies; and already they called them by no
other name than that of their bloody and
feared ministry; for, when they couldn't
avoid meeting them, they said to one another: there go the *nacas,* which means, in
our language, slaughterers or hangmen.[20]

Various of the Bethlehemites' traits may have favored their identification with the *nakaq* or, con-
versely, conferred on the *nakaq* certain particulari-
ties of these friars: dressed in long robes of rough
sackcloth, the friars wandered the city streets from
dusk into the night, ringing bells and praying for
souls in Purgatory; they frequented the roads to ask
for alms from travelers. Ultimately, it may have been
their vocation of serving in hospitals that made the
Indians suspicious. They greeted the Bethlehemite
brothers by throwing stones at them, and the historian of the order notes that a hermit who had been
confused with one of the friars met his death in this
way. Twenty or so years later, in 1747, a Bethlehemite brother was, in turn, assassinated, on the
road from Cuzco to Lima, by two Indians who took
him for a *nakaq.*[21]

Thus, at the beginning of the eighteenth century, the figure of the "slaughterer" displays more specific traits, some of which correspond to those of certain friars, themselves intermediaries (like the indigenous sorcerers) between this world and the sacred powers. No doubt not all the Spanish are *nakaq*, although virtually all of them could be: suspicions more readily rest upon a certain section of them who have, in a sense, been delegated the task of stealing fat from the Indians.

§

Curiously, the character of the slaughterer who extracts human fat can also be found, widely even today, in various regions of Spain, where, among ogres and werewolves, he is one of the protagonists in a world of frightening children's tales and legends.[22] The *sacamantecas* appears in a type of popular literature, widely disseminated at the beginning of the twentieth century, that recounts a series of grisly crimes, also referred to in carnival skits. In his study of this folk tradition, Julio Caro Baroja notes, for example, "the dismemberment of a little twelve-year-old girl in Las Hurdes of Plasencia (Cáceres)," committed by a certain José de la Iglesia, who extracted the fat from his victim in order to heal his sister, who was stricken with tuberculosis.[23] Another story connected to this theme is that of "the

double assassination and dismemberment of two
children, seven and nine years old, in Béjar, a province of Salamanca"; this crime was committed by Juan and Luisa Carricado, an "incestuous" brother and sister, in order to furnish "children's blood," recommended by a healer, to a rich man also suffering from consumption.[24] So it is not surprising to find the same type of remedy in a treatise titled *Popular Medicine in Galicia* under the article "tuberculosis": "It is said that a sorceress once even dug up a dead child, pulled out his heart, and extracted his fat in order to administer them to a person suffering from this affliction."[25]

Is there some relationship between the Spanish *sacamantecas* and the Andean *pishtako,* or is this an example of cultural parallelism? Aside from the fact that the latter explanation is only of limited interest, there seems to be no trace of the theme of the slaughterer in popular Spanish literature before the beginning of the nineteenth century.[26] Might the *sacamantecas* have been imported from America? It is not impossible that this character, in turn, may have inspired certain recent transformations in the Andean *pishtako.*

§

The versions gathered in the 1950s by Efraín Morote Best and José María Arguedas in the central regions of Peru attribute a now-classic image to the slaughterer (dark tunic, long pigsticker, magic powders, etc.) while including numerous variations.[27] While he often bears the features of a blue-eyed gringo, the *nakaq* may appear as an Indian or a mestizo, in which case he is described, significantly, as an intermediary between the indigenous milieu and the outside world. In the mid-twentieth century, however, this theme seemed more "folkloric" than anything else, even though informants occasionally indicated that such and such a well-known individual was suspected of being a *nakaq,* and that certain relatives or neighbors had been victimized. Are we dealing here with archaic beliefs, stemming from a repertory of tales and legends on their way to being forgotten? For the past ten years or so, we have observed an astonishing phenomenon: a new outbreak of rumors and panics prompted by the actions of a *nakaq* with updated characteristics.

Inquires made in the 1980s recorded a very modern use of human fat: after being exported to the United States, it serves to lubricate industrial machines, cars, airplanes, even computers, procuring enormous profits for its traffickers.[28] At the same time, another theme is spreading, that of cannibal practices: the *pishtako* isn't content just to extract the fat from his victim; he also sells his flesh, which is consumed in exclusive restaurants in Lima. According to one of the versions gathered, dismembered children of Ayacucho feed the capital.[29] The sense of fear has its counterpart in urban settings, where the slaughterers take on various, seemingly contradictory forms: thieves, rapists, terrorists, or police and military men. In the suburbs of Lima, lynchings have been reported in which the perpetrators were subjected to the punishment formerly reserved for the *pishtako* of the wild altiplano, but the crimes of individuals in uniform, wearing boots and sometimes masks, are also feared. The climate of violence sustained in Peru over the past few years by guerrillas and repression begets wild rumors: the slaughterers carry "identity cards," hold meetings, commit their crimes in groups, have formed an "organization," and are even "sent by the government."[30]

Is it by chance that a spectacular return of the *pishtako* can be observed in the region of Ayacucho, the original home of the Shining Path? In September 1987, for instance, a terrifying piece of news spread from the country to the city: five thousand slaughterers had suddenly materialized, bearing special authorization from the president of the Republic and seeking human fat in order to "pay the foreign debt" of Peru. These *nakaq* are white, bearded, dressed in long green or black coats, and armed with knives, revolvers, and even machine guns. Some of them, having been arrested by peasants and turned over to the police, were supposedly released by the authorities, who are protecting them. Others were killed by the *senderos*, which is why packs of slaughterers are now pouring back into the city, where they are seeking refuge and a continued supply of fat to provide the government with. One woman was supposedly killed in the central market bathrooms; now no one dares go there anymore, especially after dusk. The residents of several Ayacucho neighborhoods, in particular the shantytowns, are organizing to form self-defense groups: they have established night patrols in which those on duty carry whistles and torches, and burn wood fires that light up the city. Incidents are on the increase, and the victims are those reckless enough to travel far from their homes after dusk. The tension and panic reached their peak on September 11, 1987, when a young merchant from Huancayo was lynched after being accused of being a *pishtako*.[31]

Another intense panic demonstrates the presence of the slaughterer, in unprecedented forms, as far off as the popular sections of Lima. On the morning of November 30, 1988, a rumor spread that gringos armed with machine guns had entered a school, kid-

napped children, and torn out their eyes, which they
then sold abroad.[32] Hundreds of frantic mothers
rushed to the schools to collect their crying children. The most horrifying rumors escalated during
the days that followed: gringos dressed in white
smocks, again armed with machine guns, were driv-
ing around the city streets scouting for children,
their vehicle equipped with medical instruments
that enabled them to tear out eyes (in addition to
hearts or kidneys, according to certain versions), because of the need to export organs for transplants
and, once again, to pay the "foreign debt." Children
with bandaged faces, abandoned by these "eye-
extracting" doctors, had even been found on the corner of a particular street. These doctors had gone
so far as to slip envelopes containing dollar bills
into the children's pockets as payment. The ensu-
ing mass hysteria brought about several attempted
lynchings—three young French tourists were among
those threatened. Far from appeasing the population, the skeptical or ironic articles that appeared
in the press and the solemn televised denial of the
minister of health only exacerbated the feelings of
terror: what credibility do a minister's assurances
have compared with the testimony of a horrified
neighbor?

White smocks, medical technology, foreigners,

dollars: the urban slaughterer has abandoned his pigsticker, his sackcloth tunic, his little bell, his blowpipe, and his magic powders, but are we not still faced with the same rejection of and fascination with the powers that be and a certain modernity on the part of poor shantytown dwellers? It is true that the rumor of the criminal trafficking of organs, a contemporary mythical theme, occurs in many other places: Why in this case is it aimed toward children, and why their eyes? For the answer, further analyses of recent phenomena in Lima would obviously be required. It is significant that the alleged threat begins with some kind of aggression in school: Might not the resulting blindness be a physical metaphor for the darkness in which the poor and illiterate are living? The child's eyes might here represent the possibility of progress through education, an opening toward the future, and the fragile hope of a better world.[33] It is this hope that the slaughterer extinguishes.

There is no question that evidence of the *kharisiri* in Bolivia over the past few years has not reached the pitch that it has in Peru, but certain parallels seem particularly noteworthy. For instance, major scares were recorded in 1982–83 in the Northern Potosi region. They occurred in the context of a national economic crisis, aggravated by successive droughts, famine, and epidemics. The *kharisiri* made his appearance in Ocuri, among other places, a village on the road from Oruro to Sucre, where an institute for the development of agriculture and medicine had been founded with the participation of European experts.[34] Not surprisingly, we encounter a known theme once again: at the request of the World Bank, the president allegedly sent gringos on a mission to extract fat from the peasants in order to pay the foreign debt. When the red jeep from the institute is spotted traveling through the countryside, terror breaks out, the peasants run away, children stop going to school for fear of being kidnapped. Faced with threats, the foreign experts are forced to clear out.[35]

And yet we learn that the *kharisiri* who was executed in 1983 at Orinoca, and whose body was burned, was not a foreigner but a full-fledged member of the indigenous community. He had, however, placed himself on the margins of the bonds of solidarity that unite the village inhabitants: after converting to an Evangelical sect, he refused to do his part within the system of shared political and religious responsibilities. He was therefore suspected of having made a pact with the devil, who had enabled him to grow rich and buy a van, which he used for personal business. Thus he appeared to be an extension of the outside world inside the village and, worse still, a traitor who had put himself at the service of foreigners. The discovery of dollar bills in his home only confirmed his criminal activities as a *kharisiri,* and his association with the others. This otherness was absolute, for the punishment inflicted upon him (the refusal of a burial) excluded him definitively from humanity.[36]

§

If by definition the *kharisiri* incarnates a vision of the other associated with evil (but still human) forces, it is understandable that he would be capable of both continuity over the centuries and of assuming a variety of forms, changing according to local circumstances and the particular moment in history. Yet at the conclusion of this rapid overview, we notice an evolution in the Andean process of imagining the foreigner. At the time of the Taqui Ongo, following the European invasion, the other is identified, in the aggregate, with the Spaniards who, appearing from a previously unsuspected outside world, came to impose domination, thereby provoking brutal ruptures in the indigenous community. As time went by, this representation of the other covered a more limited field, while giving rise to an archetypical figure, many of whose traits were inspired by those of certain religious groups (notably Bethlehemites) of the colonial period. The *kharisiri* at the time acted individually, as if delegated power from the dominant authorities. In recent manifestations his traits have been updated, and now bear characteristics of an advanced modernity: those of doctors, engineers, or terrorists. And particularly in Ayacuchok, the return of a collective image of the *kharisiri* has been noted, with the irruption of packs of slaughterers who strike according to a supposed government plan. The example of Orinoca (and of Chipaya) illustrate another no less remarkable evolution, which in some sense corresponds to an interiorization of this otherness, since in these cases the *kharisiri*, though connected to the vast network of the outside world, hails from the indigenous milieu. This is certainly a symptom of a profound crisis: the intrusion of modernity into the heart of Andean communities threatens the very roots of their identities.

FIVE

Gregorio's Troubles

IN 1978, FIVE YEARS BEFORE THE TRAGEDY AT ORI-
noca, the village of Chipaya had been shaken by the
kharisiri affair: that the "guilty parties" in this case
managed to escape punishment resulted from an exceptional combination of circumstances (Gregorio's
brother-in-law's appeal for help and the last-minute
arrival of a military detachment). But was it a coincidence that the drama occurred during a particularly critical moment in Chipaya history? Apart
from the internal divisions that threatened the unity
of each *ayllu*, we know that there were heated conflicts in the village caused by the growth of new religious movements (Catechist, Evangelical, Pentecostal) over the previous twelve years or so. Two ways of
thinking were in opposition: on the one hand, the
"pagans" were indignant at the abandonment of a
tradition which was all the more venerable as it appeared to them to have been respected since time immemorial; on the other hand, the brothers were
setting a precedent for a radical split by rejecting
customs they considered to be diabolical. For a long
time, the initially marginal pioneers of the new cults
were condemned, even persecuted, by the other inhabitants of the village. But the rapid progress of the
new religions resulted in a reversal of the balance of

power by the end of the 1970s, the pagans becoming a minority relative to the brothers of the three religious orders.

The village then underwent a mutation. For several years the *alcaldes* had had trouble coming up with a list of "volunteers" to sponsor religious festivals (choosing me as *pasante* of the Kiliminti festival was no doubt symptomatic). After 1978, the traditional system of *cargos*, which formed the backbone of the Chipayas' social organization, came crashing down. During my previous stay I was able to record the dates of some of the last festivals celebrated in the village: in 1977 *mallku* Kemperani; in 1978 Kiliminti, San Gerónimo, and Guadalupe; in 1980 the *mallku* of the Lauca river and Santa Ana herself. And I have mentioned the tumult that affected religious structures, visibly transforming the village, and even the surrounding landscape: the alters at the four corners of the church square had disappeared, as well as the Rosario chapel; most of the stations of the cross, which had extended outward in four directions in rhythm with the flatness of Chipaya space, had been destroyed. The new extirpation of idolatries being carried out by the brothers, three centuries after the first, was weakening the religious syncretism that had traditionally given order to the Chipayas' representation of the world. The first Pentecostal temple had been built in the village in 1976, the first Evangelical temple in 1979, and during this time the Catechists were taking control of the church. The last pagans, who were now marginalized (mainly in the Camichiri district), had only the chapels of Santiago and Geronimo, which were practically in ruins, at their disposal.

Thus a long phase in the history of Chipaya was ending right before my eyes. The *kharisiri* drama fits into this juncture—the end of a particular world—and is only one expression of the crisis sweeping the village at that moment. We are therefore tempted to interpret the affair as a defensive reaction on the part of the traditionalists faced with the intrusion of the outside world. This reading could be corroborated by the fact that the two young men from Ayparavi belonged to the Pentecostal church, and by the interest Gregorio had already expressed in the Catechist movement (which he officially joined after his persecution). A more detailed examination of the events of 1978 shows that such an interpretation, though not entirely inaccurate, fails to take into account a far more complex reality. The inquiry that was conducted, drawing information both from Gregorio and from other informants, reveals that the leaders of the frenzied mob in fact belonged to all the religious groups of Chipaya: whether Catechist or Evangelical, pagan or Pentecostal, all were convinced of the *kharisiris'* guilt. It's true that the *alcalde* of Aransaya, Honorio L., and of Manasaya, my compadre Felipe P., were at the time both associated with the pagan group, and that they were the ones who took the initiative to file suit with the higher authorities in the name of the Chipayas for a "crime against the public welfare"; they were the ones zealous enough to travel to Oruro to denounce the actions of the *kharisiris*. But Gregorio's accusers also included a good number of Pentecostals, who didn't hesitate to persecute the brothers they considered dangerous renegades. Thus a curious alliance of antagonistic religious groups was formed to punish the vampires.

§

Why choose Gregorio as the main culprit? His sympathy for the Catechists at a time when they were becoming a majority in Chipaya is not enough to explain his exclusion from the community. In fact, he had several personal stigmas that designated him as a potential scapegoat. He was marginal, so to speak, from birth: an illegitimate child, abandoned by his mother when she married, he was treated like an orphan and raised by his grandfather. His grandfather's death, while Gregorio was still an adolescent, left him alone, penniless, and reduced to

extreme poverty with no family to turn to. He managed to establish a household but couldn't stand living with his exploitative father-in-law and decided
to work abroad. From this point the course of his life
could only generate envy and suspicion: starting
with nothing, he gets rich, and manages to obtain a
certain degree of comfort. How? Most Chipayas
temporarily migrate to the Chilean valleys. Com-
mercial activity, on the other hand, is far less com-
mon: by opening a "shop" in his home and by
scouring the countryside for business, Gregorio
only accentuated his uniqueness. Was he a good
member of the community? He claims to have assid-
uously executed the *faenas,* the collective work obli-
gations, but many (partial?) witnesses assert the
contrary. And while over the years he took on a
number of community responsibilities, it turns out
that they didn't follow the traditional pattern:
working with the school administration or the peasant union was new to the village. On this point,
Antonio's confession suggests a probably biased interpretation: according to him, these duties show
the Chipayas' confidence in Gregorio and his integration into the community. But if we look at it from
another perspective, don't they also point to an ac-
celeration of the village's integration into national
life and of the changes brought on by the encroach-

ment of the modern world, of which Gregorio became an agent?

The accusation of vampirism is therefore directed at an individual who by birth and life experience is distinct from other members of his group. This singularity must also be seen against a backdrop of permanent conflicts and hatred, all the more vicious as it involves close relatives. For it is within his own family that Gregorio counts his worst enemies, even though, as we saw, the scope of this enmity is limited. First, there is Pedro, his brother-in-law (and my *compadre*). The respective *estancias* of the two men, Takata and Yunguyo, are contiguous, so that there is constant quarreling over the boundaries of pastures or trespassing animals. When Pedro gets drunk, which happens frequently, he takes it out on his brother and threatens to kill him; the latter's complaints go unheeded by the authorities. Gregorio's second persecutor is none other than his half-brother, Antonio, born legitimately after their mother's marriage. As Gregorio tells the story, in order to live peacefully with Antonio he invited him to move to the Yunguyo *estancia* and to share the land. But Antonio happens also to be Pedro's son-in-law, and the two of them are now combining forces to evict Gregorio from his own *estancia*. Gregorio is thus finding his best intentions turning against him;

his brother's betrayal is the bitterest wound of all. He later explained to me that it was not only because of his animals that he had had to go to his land the Sunday of our appointment (the day before his confession); a more serious problem was on his mind. With Antonio's backing, Pedro had undertaken the construction of a hut that encroached on Yunguyo's land. When Gregorio complained, the three got into a fist fight.

I had known Antonio since my first visits. He was always very warm when we met, though he wasn't a regular informant. It was disturbing to discover such hatred between people with whom I was on friendly terms. After Gregorio's confession, I naturally began seeking out Antonio's company. Did he suspect that I was interested in him for a reason? Did he follow the example of his father-in-law, to whom I was linked by a *compadrazgo* relationship? He too asked me to become his son's godfather. How could I refuse? There's no question he too had other motivations, but there was something touching about the attention he paid to me, the graciousness with which he offered me cheeses and eggs. For my part, when I offered him gifts or when we had friendly chats together, I once again felt uneasy in spite of myself; in responding to Antonio's benevolent gaze, I couldn't help thinking about the violent disputes

between the two brothers, and I too seemed to be be-
traying Gregorio.

At the heart of the *kharisiri* affair, then, is a narrow circle of enemy brothers and brothers-in-law,
whose conflicts seem essentially to be inspired by
prosaic, even sordid interests. To what extent do religious differences come into play? Pedro and Antonio
are members of the traditionalist group, but not without certain nuances: Antonio seems halfhearted in
matters of religion, almost agnostic; Pedro is a *yatiri*
and fortune-teller, and although his convictions are
fundamentally pagan, by the time of the affair his
wife had already converted to Pentecostalism, so
that he found himself more or less constrained to
follow her, despite his reticence. He too was therefore experiencing a personal drama, which probably
exacerbated his aggressiveness. In his own manner,
tormented and almost schizophrenic, Pedro incarnates that strange alliance between pagans and Pentecostals that we observed earlier among Gregorio's
persecutors. Family feuds and personal tragedies
were among the many seemingly minor items that
found themselves amplified by the divisions that had
long disrupted the village, helping to bring about the
major, public crisis of the *kharisiris*.

The one essential missing link in the sequence of
the drama is something I discovered only during the

last week of my stay. During his travels, Gregorio
had established a connection with a member of the
Challacota community, Mario T., with whom he
had a business relationship. In 1978 this trading
partner was also accused of the crime of *kharisiri* in
his village. He was the one who supposedly organized the sale of blood abroad, thus maintaining the
link to the outside world. How did the crisis play
itself out in Challacota? To find out, another inquiry would have to have been performed on site.
According to my Chipaya informants, Mario, like
Gregorio, was almost lynched; in the end he had to
flee his village and never went back. Further, an important detail suggests a previously unsuspected dimension to the affair: back in the 1950s, Mario's
grandfather had also been accused of being a *kharisiri,* and had been slain. Gregorio's partner therefore
also bore a distinctive stigma, in this case a fateful
heredity: this grandfather allegedly taught him the
practice of vampirism, and transmitted his inclina-
tion for crime. As the plot thickens, the roots of the
problem recede into the past: we don't know in what
way this grandfather distinguished himself from the
rest of his community. At least we're on the track of
family lines of *kharisiris,* or reputed *kharisiris,* similar to certain lines of *yatiris* or sorcerers. Through
Mario, the unfortunate Gregorio was connected not

only to the outside world but to another unlucky
precedent.

Indeed, Gregorio seems to attract misfortune. This fits in with psychological characteristics that are primarily those of a loser: despite (or because of) his success in business, he was put down by this village milieu with which he never managed to become fully integrated. Did his abandoned childhood cause him to become inept in human relationships? He nonetheless turns his "persecution" into a virtue: we saw, in his story, that he has reinterpreted the events of his life in light of the life of Christ. He too was martyred and considers his suffering, in retrospect, as a sign of being "chosen." God condemned him to live a life of misery here on earth, but his innocence assures his salvation. After his ordeal, he joined the Catechist group definitively, the only support he received having come from the Oblate fathers, and he has become part of a community in which he can be recognized as a "brother," equal to all other members. There is no doubt that he is a sincere follower of the faith, experiencing it as pain, which he embraces and is sanctified by.

Will a gruesome destiny befall Gregorio's entire family? Remember that his two sons became idiots as a result of the abuse they received at the time of the affair. The story of his youngest daughter is no less sinister. After we left Chipaya, I found myself with Gregorio in Oruro, in a waiting room at the law courts, to which we had come in search of documents relating to the inquiry previously conducted on *kharisiris*. (To my great disappointment, if not surprise, I learned they had all disappeared.) At this point a woman passed by, dressed as a *chola*; Gregorio nervously hestitated to greet her. "Do you know that woman?" I asked. He told me that she used to live in Huachacalla with her husband. Recall that at the time of the affair, Gregorio's wife was pregnant; after fleeing to Huachacalla, she gave birth to a little girl. The woman in question, seeing the distress of the parents, offered to adopt the child, and they gratefully accepted the offer. A few years later, however, the woman left her husband to live with another man, in Oruro, and took the little girl with her. But the man spent his time drinking. Three months before the encounter in the waiting room he had raped Gregorio's daughter, who was now about ten years old. Gregorio demanded that the woman give him back his daughter, to whom she had provided such inadequate care. The woman agreed to give her back but demanded to be paid the cost of ten years' "room and board." As a result, Gregorio was in the middle of a lawsuit with the woman (not so much for the rape as for the money).

It was also in Oruro that Gregorio, recalling his
childhood memories, told me about another of his
misfortunes, which according to him left a profound
mark. He was about twelve years old when he lost
his grandmother. Shortly thereafter, his grandfather
began living with another woman, who became
something of a wicked stepmother to Gregorio. She
had a son of about the same age, and Gregorio soon
became his scapegoat. One night, this childhood
companion "stole" his own belongings and hid
them by burying them in the cemetery; he was so vicious he even wore Gregorio's sandals, so that the
footprints would make Gregorio look guilty. Indeed, a scandal broke out, in keeping with this
Machiavellian plan: despite his protestations (even
at that early age) of innocence, Gregorio was accused of stealing. Faced with the evidence, he was
humiliated by being publicly forced to ask forgiveness.

Whether this was exactly the way things happened or not hardly matters: this at least was the
narrator's memory, and his interpretation. I ventured to ask him who this childhood companion
was, the true guilty party. "It's Fortunato L!" I was
stupefied to learn that Gregorio's first persecutor
was one of my close friends, a member of the group
that had accompanied me on my visit to the Mu-

ratos, the Urus of Lake Poopo. I didn't see Fortunato during my last stay in Chipaya: he was in prison in Oruro, accused of appropriating a large sum of money that had been given to the village by a charitable organization. Was justice finally served?

§

Why did Gregorio finally tell me of his problems and ask for my help? One might have expected him to turn to the priest, since he was a member of the Catechists. When I asked him this question, he explained that he was involved in a conflict with them as well. The disagreement had to do with his oldest daughter, who for some time had been living with a man (a first step toward marriage for the Chipayas), and had recently given birth. But she didn't get along with her companion, who beat her and who also refused to recognize the child as his own. She therefore wanted to separate from her concubinary, a plan Gregorio approved of: "Let her come back to my house with her baby, she'll be happier." The priest, however, was hostile to the "divorce" and was urging the couple to stay together and marry in a religious ceremony. "I can't go to the priest," explained Gregorio, "because he disapproves of my advice to my daughter, and anyway, he wouldn't believe me."

Thus I was Gregorio's only recourse. How was it

that I seemed to him the most qualified person to help? It is understandable, given the nature of the crime of which he was accused, that he would go to a foreigner who is at the same time separate from the other gringos. Although I do represent the otherness whose grip reaches all the way to Chipaya, I am not just any foreigner: I've been known here for a long time, I have many *compadres* and friends. Having sponsored Kiliminti in the past has contributed to my integration in the village, and because of my research the Chipayas themselves consult me as an expert in matters of Uru history. I think I can say that I occupy an ecumenical position with regard to the different groups who are in conflict, as well as that of an intermediary between Chipaya and the outside world. My unique situation was no doubt apparent to Gregorio when he came to ask my help. He was basically saying: "The Chipayas accuse me of selling you their blood. Therefore you're the one, with all that you represent here, who can save me. I beg you to exercise your power in my favor."

The power I have at my disposal rests on the fact that ultimately I belong to the world of the rich and the privileged. The feast I offered during the celebration of the Kiliminti was certainly far less sumptuous than that of many other *pasantes,* but they were grateful to me for making the effort to come from such a distant country to fulfill my commitments. The Chipayas also know that I mix with powerful people in La Paz, such as the director of the Anthropology Museum, and that in some sense I participate in this power, as was evidenced by the supply-filled truck which arrived in the village all those years ago. And even though I don't travel by personal airplane, like certain missionaries, my possessions bespeak my wealth: the gas burner, the cans of Nescafé, the inexhaustible supplies of cigarettes, the candles, the sleeping bag, even my personal belongings (my shoes, in particular, are highly coveted). I am often asked, "How much does a plane ticket from France to Bolivia cost?" What can I say? I can't lie, but telling the truth doesn't make sense either: in the context of Chipaya, the amount, translated into pesos, is astronomical, totally unimaginable. I can stress that my ticket is paid for by my university all I want: I must be very important if mysterious institutions would grant me such funds.

So I am aware that the esteem the Chipayas have for me is based on their obligatory deference for a representative of the dominant world (even though I am sure of the sincere, and reciprocated, friendship of some of them). There is no question that my research benefited from this relationship of dominance; despite the consideration I tried to show my informants, we were all caught up in a mechanism that was imposed from without and was difficult to surmount even in very close relationships. The basic inequality in our status constantly left its mark on the various phases of my inquiry, even on the very last one, Gregorio's call for help. It is quite true that the anthropologist, inevitably taking advantage of his privileges, and gathering information which he then delivers to the outside world, performs the work, metaphorically, of a vampire. Gregorio was therefore very perceptive to tell me of his martyrdom and to ask me for help: he had recognized me, if not as a colleague (since he was, in fact, innocent), at least as someone likely to understand him, for, though I was god for a day, I was also something of a *kharisiri*.

Six

Religious Quests

PARADOXICAL AS IT MAY SEEM, THE EXTREMELY tense climate that characterized the end of my stay, and the revelation of much interpersonal hatred, did not throw into question my first impression, which was that the collective conflicts that had been stirring up the village so long and so violently have, over the last decade, more or less calmed down. The crisis struck, a number of century-old institutions crumbled, but then the history of Chipaya entered into a phase of recomposition and readjustment, of compromise even, through which, if not a new order, at least a modus vivendi was sought. How did the inhabitants of the village survive the crisis socially? It's as if, disconcerted and disoriented by the changes of 1978–82, they no longer recognize themselves and are trying to establish other guideposts, and in so doing are starting on the path of reconciliation. The earlier devastation essentially taught the different groups the need for mutual acceptance, for certain conventions that ended up being more or less tacitly restored—in short, for a religious truce. Will this be at the price of new exclusions if the threatened revival of the *kharisiri* affair actually occurs? Much remains uncertain.

106   The history of Chipaya has followed a rather dif-

ferent course from the one I would have imagined at the end of my stay in 1982. At that time, one might have supposed that, in a continuation of the previous evolution, the new religious movements would continue their expansion to the point of totally eliminating pagan beliefs. The reality turned out to be more complex and nuanced. Though earlier customs will never regain their former primacy, they are nonetheless experiencing a partial revival, while the Protestant churches—Pentecostal and particularly Evangelical—are experiencing a marked decline. Ultimately, it is the Catechists and, even more broadly, the Catholics who are now dominant in Chipaya, as much in number (more than two-thirds of the population) as in influence. Did the presence of the priest, who has been living in the village for five years (and for the first time since its foundation), enable the Roman church to consolidate in this way? His actions were no doubt instrumental. But the historical and ethnic singularity of the Chipayas also came into play. The neighboring villages of Sabaya and Huachacalla, for instance, are still dominated by a strong Protestant majority. Chipaya therefore stands out not only as an Uru enclave in the midst of a vast Aymara zone, but also as a Catholic enclave. Are the Chipayas trying to affirm their identity in the religious domain?

Every Sunday, I conscientiously explore the site of worship. Outside of feast days dedicated to a particular saint, I had never, on earlier visits, seen such crowds in the church: each week more than eighty people squeeze in, even when the priest isn't there (as when he's visiting other villages). It's still the same adobe edifice—modest, well kept, regularly whitewashed, and now covered with a corrugated metal roof; but the inside is unrecognizable: there is not a single image, no statues of Santiago, Guadalupe, or even Santa Ana, patron saint of Chipaya. They've all disappeared. Aside from a naked cross that stands out against the bare wall above the altar, there is nothing to distinguish the interior from that of a Protestant church. It is particularly packed on the Sunday immediately preceding All Saints' Day, October 29; this attendance no doubt has something to do with the distribution of aid (rice, sugar, etc.) scheduled for that afternoon, part of "Project Children." That morning, before mass, the priest appears in shirtsleeves and blue jeans, making preparations, walking purposefully back and forth from the altar to the corner that serves as sacristy. He then publicly dons a chasuble and sacerdotal ornaments, and, after a few words of introduction, two or three Catechist assistants read a series of verses. Haltingly they plow through the story of the Pharisee and the

publican. The faithful listen attentively, but how
much do they understand?

When I arrive at the Evangelical chapel, I find no more than thirty people in attendance (about a dozen men and fifteen women). The building is smaller than the church, but it too had been packed during my 1982 visit, the followers overflowing into the street. The Evangelical group was more dynamic at the time; it was the church whose membership swelled the fastest. I remember how self-assured the Evangelicals were by the success of their proselytizing, and although their prayers remain fervent, I now sense, in the sparse attendance and the attitudes and expressions, a kind of disenchantment. For over the past few years, the Evangelicals have also experienced the highest rate of defection. This dwindling is alleged to be caused by internal differences and personal rivalries; I was also told stories of adultery which supposedly weakened the faith of certain followers. There is no question, however, that the decline of the Evangelical group is the almost automatic result of religious competition, and that most of the defectors returned to the Catholic church.

While the Pentecostal group hasn't grown in several years, it is doing better at resisting the flood of defections. The chapel regularly attracts almost forty faithfuls (about fifteen men and twenty women).

This stability can no doubt be attributed to their strong cohesiveness, to the particularly warm ties among the brothers, and basically to the intensity of their messianic quest. Also, after the priest set up residence in Chipaya, a pastor from Sabaya came to live there as well. On Sunday he holds service dressed in a flame-blue three-piece suit with a low-cut U-shaped vest, along with a matching light blue shirt and a gray-blue, impeccably knotted tie. When he reads verses, he hesitates and stumbles, so he too prefers to have them read by an assistant, after which he offers free, somewhat questionable interpretations. But the pastor is at ease with improvisation: he is remarkably eloquent, his voice swells with inspiration, rises to a resounding pitch, subsides into harmonious inflections, falls back, carefully measuring out a weighty silence, then picks up, swells again, the stops punctuated by the refrain: "No es cierto verdad?" Finally, his body trembling, almost in a trace, the orator invokes the Holy Spirit, transporting the faithfuls, who respond with exalted *Gloria Dios*.

§

Near the beginning of my stay, wandering the village alleyways on the Manasaya side, I see Cornelio M. again, sitting on his patio. I call out to him and he stands up to greet me, apparently surprised: "How do you know my name?" "What do you mean, don't you recognize me?" Cornelio becomes effusive; once again I am in the presence of his familiar warm smile, his prominent canines, but now I'm the one who's surprised: when I knew him before, he was a young and ardent Pentecostal; now he is tottering before me, speaking huskily. How is it possible? Despite his hazy consciousness he is aware of my astonishment, and apologizes for having been drinking: this year he is *alcalde* and so is obliged to participate in the customs of the fields. A little while later he asks me (as so many others have done) to become his son's godfather. This intrigues me even more, since *compadrazgo* now has certain "pagan" connotations in Chipaya.

I often worked with Cornelio in 1973 and 1974: aside from being a clear and precise informant, he served as an intermediary to his grandfather, Mateo, one of the oldest men in the village (I remember his hunched-over silhouette and his limp). Mateo was himself the grandson of Anacleto M., who, forty years earlier, had been one of Alfred Métraux's informants. I don't know if he said it to make me happy, but Mateo claimed he vaguely remembered a gringo like me staying in the village, who was interested in the customs. As for Cornelio, he was a perfect collaborator when it came to irrigation techniques or questions of family trees, but when I asked

him questions about the *mallkus,* the sacrifices or
ritual tables, he grew distant, joked and laughed un-
comfortably. It was apparent to me that his interpretations weren't trustworthy. Which is why the
change is so striking when, a few days after our reu-
nion, now sober, he explains to me that he fulfills
his duties as an *alcalde* by carefully respecting all
the customs, "as before." And he enumerates them
obligingly: the carnival, the sowing, capturing the
winds, and so forth. True, the monuments in which
the *mallkus* reside have been destroyed, but he makes
certain to mention them by name in his prayers,
"in memory" (*para recordar*). The tenderness with
which he evokes each *mallku* and the slightest detail
of their costumes contrasts strangely with his previous detached attitude. And when I mention Mateo, the grandfather to whom he was so devoted, I
see the same look of tenderness in his eyes, mixed
with a touch of sadness.

Has Cornelio lost the Pentecostal faith? He speaks
to me very openly about his religious itinerary. The
story of his conversion, twenty years ago, follows
the classic model: his young child was sick, they
tried all the remedies and consulted all the healers in
vain. Then came the revelation: this affliction meant
he should follow the path of the Lord, which he did,
and his son recovered. In the 1970s, Cornelio was
thus one of the pioneers of the Pentecostal church in

Chipaya. The persecution the brothers experienced,

but also the hardships of life in this desolate pampa, prompted him to emigrate to warmer climates: he moved to the colony of Yapacani, near Santa Cruz, where other families had preceded him. Years passed (which is why I hadn't seen Cornelio for so long); they were happy years until his wife, in turn, fell sick. All the remedies failed, she was even taken to the hospital in Oruro and grew worse and worse until she died. This misfortune profoundly afflicted Cornelio, who sank into hopeless melancholy and began drinking. He couldn't go on living in Yapacani, so he returned to Chipaya. But his faith had been shaken, he no longer went to church. After a while he remarried and returned to the customs, to the extent that the transformations that had occurred in the village allowed.

It was this same Cornelio who, as *alcalde* of Manasaya, had called a gathering of members of the *ayllu* in order to sound an alert on a new threat of *kharisiris*. His second wife was ill, stricken with fever, and complained of suspicious spots on her chest. He remained evasive in response to my careful questions.

§

Martin's itinerary seems typical of that of many Chipayas. In 1982 I found out that he'd converted two years earlier to the Evangelical faith, which, for a man so erudite in matters of rites and customs, might seem surprising. But in Martin, whose personality combines a natural apprehensiveness with a questioning religious sense, these fluctuations apparently reflect the collective currents that are sweeping Chipaya. He told me the circumstances of this conversion: his wife's illness and the dream of his "visit to God."[37] Seven years later, though, Martin smiles knowingly and shows no embarrassment in telling me that he no longer goes to chapel on Sunday but to church: he's a Catholic again.

A Catholic, and not a Catechist. We noted earlier a distinction between the two terms: "Catechist" still designates the brothers who, in response to the Protestant competition, preach a religion cleansed of all remnants of paganism, while "Catholic" tends to encompass those who recognize the Roman church yet allow themselves to practice customs, to varying degrees, which they themselves have revised. Does this distinction paradoxically indicate (in contradiction with the Catechist doctrine) a return to a traditional Catholicism that might be said to function essentially as a cover, beneath a more or less intact veneer, for pagan-Christian syncretism? Not exactly, for the syncretic system that combined the worship of saints and of *mallkus* in a series of collective holidays has fallen apart with the abandonment

of the religious *cargos* previously assured by the *pasantes*. By an unexpected twist, this very disappearance brought on a new era, a kind of redemption, conferring on what remains of the customs a new legitimacy. The customs have been amended, "reformed" say the informants themselves, that is, cleansed of their blatantly idolatrous tendencies—the wayside crosses dedicated to the saints and especially the monuments dedicated to the *mallkus* (all the oratories, at their sacred sites, have been destroyed). As a result, no one in Chipaya, not even Vicente Guarachi, calls himself a "pagan" anymore. But while they may resign themselves to eliminating the *cargo* system, how can they help but pray for generous rain, good crops, or healthy animals? A number of apparently fundamental customs—those dealing with cultivated lands and fertility—are in fact kept alive, though in a reinterpreted form.

Martin now performs the duties of an officiant (*sukachiri*) in Aransaya; he is responsible for overseeing the rituals intended to protect the fields and obtain good harvests. Pleased to see me taking copious notes, as before, he explains at length how the new customs work. Adapted to the new religious order, these customs are characterized by an obvious simplification (one might say impoverishment if one tended toward nostalgic conservatism), but they are hardly any different, in their basic principles, from the former practices. The agrarian rituals are still in the hands of the field guardians (the *kamayos*), generally in collaboration with the *alcalde*. Their principal phases, although fewer, are the same as before: the opening of the fields in October before sowing, their closing after the sowing time, the Carnival cycle during their maturation, the passing of command in April, after the harvest. The main difference, with respect to the former customs, is at the moment of closing the fields: the *mallku* (called *skalkontavi*), which in the past stood in the middle of the cultivated field, is no longer erected; instead, in the same location, a "table" (*mesa*) is set up with clumps of earth. In front of the *mesa* an animal is sacrificed, incense and copal are burnt, and drink offerings made of ritual ingredients are scattered. With the disappearance of the *skalkontavi* the three *tishñe* are no longer celebrated, in the course of which, on three successive Saturdays, the guardians and the officiant buried several dozen *tchua* (little cones made with animal fat) throughout the cultivated field. But if the *mallku* of the fields no longer exists, the composition of the ingredients continues to follow unchanging rules, and offerings are made to the powers above as well as to those below. We know that the incense is intended for the saints, and the copal for the *mallkus* as well as for Pachamama, the Earth Mother (who is present in as many *Virgenes** as in designated places). Reduced to six shallow cups, the table preserves the essence of the pagan-Christian system's ritual thought: there are mineral powders (*sebarios*) for the *mallkus* and the *samiris, llumpaja* (ground white corn) for the Pachamama, and *kulli* (ground black corn) for the Sky. The agrarian rituals are still intended to mediate between above and below, right and left, masculine and feminine, in order to put the sacred powers in contact with one another and to bring about the beneficial conjunction of the Sky and the Earth. And the ritual voices still and always speak of gifts: a good harvest occurs in exchange for what the men have offered the gods, or God in his many forms. There may well be theological uncertainty, but this in no way affects the primary necessity, for man, of giving.

The cycle of agrarian rituals culminates with the Carnival, the only collective festival the Chipayas continue to celebrate. It no longer begins on Saturday as it used to, which was the day of the *mallkus*, but on Sunday, with the gathering of members of the

*The virgins (not to be confused with the Virgin Mary) who protect a given place. See Wachtel, *Le Retour des ancêtres* (note 1, below), 64–65.—Trans.

two *ayllus,* the two *alcaldes* in the lead, in front of the church tower, decorated as before with bread and streamers. Animals are no longer sacrificed on top of the tower, but offerings are made with the ritual ingredients, followed by dancing and drinking contests. On Monday, the *kamayos* symbolically give the first ears of quinoa to their *alcalde,* who distributes them on Tuesday to each member of his moiety as a promise of luck and a symbol of belonging to the community. And until Wednesday, the authorities and the *kamayos* host one ceremonial meal (*alsa*) after another, bringing the Chipayas together in an affirmation of their identity.

The Carnival celebration, traditionally hosted by the *alcaldes,* raised a key question: whether the authorities should participate in the festival. For a long time the brothers, whether Catechist, Evangelical, or Pentecostal, refused to be compromised by pagan practices. On this point, significant changes have diminished religious tensions in Chipaya over the past few years, either because the Chipayas have grown weary of the endless conflicts between rival groups or because a series of bad harvests has led them to the idea of hedging their bets by observing as many rituals as possible, from all the religious options. The two *ayllus* held meetings in which the question of the role of the authorities with respect to the

"modern" customs was debated. Agreements were
finally reached that made it obligatory for the *al-caldes* to participate. The brothers of the three faiths now tolerate this participation: when someone assumes the function of *alcalde,* he is given a year's leave from the church in order to fulfill his duties. This happens "in principle," they add, for no one is compelled: everyone has some leeway—to participate in a few or in many customs?—at his own risk, or more precisely at the risk of the community. In other words, a degree of personal freedom is being recognized.

One of the most noticeable results of the religious transformations in Chipaya is the accentuation (and recognition) of the personal dimension of beliefs, including belief in the customs. The new movements introduced a concept of religion centered on faith and the concern for individual salvation, hence their radical opposition to the ancient pagan-Christian system, which was structured around the rotation of *cargos* and communal organization. Paradoxically, then, the brothers' greatest triumph is to have instilled this sense of individualization into religion, which has worked its way down to those practices and beliefs considered to be pagan. Other turn-abouts resulted. There is no longer a festival of the *mallkus,* but those who continue to be devoted to these ancient tutelary powers can still, when a particular *mallku*'s day arrives, pray to that *mallku* individually, within themselves (as Cornelio does when he honors them "in memory"). Even for the traditionalists, religious worship is only a step away from becoming a private affair. The growth in popularity of certain practices considered to be pagan is perhaps favored by this previously contentious idea of liberty.

The return to the home, to the nuclear family, is apparent elsewhere, outside the religious domain, even in architectural changes in the village. When the houses were round and scattered, one could easily pass from one to another without obstruction; they were separated only by low walls (on which one could sit and talk). For several years now, the walls have been getting higher and higher. The houses are becoming better and better aligned, and their owners are now surrounding them with walls almost the height of a man, which isolate them from their neighbors. The relationships among village dwellers are visibly marked by the growing individualism.

Thus various factors converge: the weakening of Protestant groups, the consolidation of the Catechists and the Catholics, the participation of the brothers in the "reformed" customs, the personalization of faith, a rash of defections, or rather of criss-

crossing from one group to another, and an increasingly individualistic style of life have resulted in
greater toleration of religious differences. At the
same time, the reinstatement of the customs (at least
relative to previous years) among both Catholics
and Protestants diminishes their differences and
tends toward homogenization. The iconoclast war
has been replaced by a religious truce.

§

On Friday, October 13, as I was wandering around
on the Aransaya side, whom should I see but Vicente
Guarachi, standing at the foot of his doorway,
drunk, his head drooping, wearing a "Korean" cap,
urinating very ostentatiously in front of two young
women, who are both embarrassed and curious. He
greets me warmly despite his foggy state of mind. I
visit him the next day. His cluttered house suggests a
certain level of comfort: a wooden armchair (in
which Vicente invites me to sit), a sewing machine,
an impressive radio–tape player, a large gas stove, a
real bed (on which my host sits). On the wall, curiously, is a pretty poster depicting the lush Maryland
countryside.

Peppering his words, as usual, with sarcastic
laughter, Vicente explains to me that he no longer
lives regularly in Chipaya; during a good part of the
year he lives in Oruro, where he conducts his appar-

ently lucrative activities as a *yatiri*. I'm aware that he
has a tendency to be egotistical: "People consult me
from all over!" He gives me his exact address, invit-
ing me to visit him in the city. His comments on
Chipaya are cynical, pessimistic: "The village is
going to disappear, it's over." He is obviously referring to the village as it was years ago, its life permeated by customs. In those days the Chipayas who
had emigrated to distant places returned at least
once a year for the Santa Ana festival; now there is
no longer a festival, and they never come back. So
Vicente claims to have lost interest in the village: he
feels he's done enough for it (he even assumed the
post of *corregidor* once again last year). He is no
longer demanding that Camichiri be upgraded to a
canton. But he continues to defend the division of
the Aransaya *ayllu* into four sections: the fields are
larger, the harvests more abundant. But what about
the droughts, the pigs' demise? All the Chipayas'
misfortunes are due to the anger of the *mallkus*
and the saints, who have been pitifully abandoned.
Vicente goes on to speak disparagingly of the Catechists, the Evangelicals, the Pentecostals, and finally
the priest. When I ask him about the 1978 *kharisiri*
affair, he provides few details, as much out of dis-
cretion, it seems to me, as out of concern to main-
tain dignity: since the affair brings no honor to the
village, he prefers not to talk about it. I know, in

fact, that he wasn't among the persecutors of the accused. And I have the satisfaction of finding out that
Vicente, whom I always held in high esteem and had
friendly feelings toward, to this day defends the unfortunate Gregorio.

In the course of our discussion I learn something
that disturbs and confuses me: last year, as *corregidor,* Vicente received a visit from Daniel Muricio,
the "president" of the Urus Moratos of Lake Poopo.
He was looking for Martin, Benito, and Fortunato,
who had accompanied me in 1974 when I met Daniel for the first time at the *estancia* of Llapallapani, as
well as two years later when we visited the Urus-Itus
of Desaguadero. Unfortunately my friends were not
in Chipaya at the time, and I can imagine how disappointed Daniel must have been. Especially, Vicente
adds, as he had made the journey because he wanted
Chipaya teachers to come live on the banks of Lake
Poopo and teach the Puquina language to the Urus
Moratos. I can picture the scene in Llapallapani and
wonder what role I played in this dream of Daniel's:
his nostalgia for the ancestors' language reverber-
ates back to me.

§

I wanted to have a conversation with father Ramon,
the priest in Chipaya, but after the national holiday
of October 12, I saw him only occasionally, from a

distance; we greeted each other cordially, but he seemed to be avoiding me. His house (which is made of bricks) was only fifty meters or so away from Santiago's, so we were basically neighbors. I expected him to take the first step, but I waited in vain: he was being decidedly reserved. After a good two weeks, I vowed to keep an eye out for him (yet another one I was on the lookout for); one afternoon, seeing him leave the school surrounded by a group of students, I rushed over, exchanged a few polite remarks, and invited him to my house "for coffee." He seemed extremely surprised and excused himself, saying he had an enormous amount of work; when I insisted, he promised to "cross the street" in an hour. Two hours later, when he still hadn't shown up, I ventured to knock on his door and practically kidnapped him.

So now father Ramon is sitting in front of me on the bench. He drinks coffee in moderation and doesn't smoke. His easy smile is accompanied by a distant attitude. He declares, abruptly, that he is wondering why I want to talk to him, and openly admits his distrust of anthropologists, from whom he's read some questionable works that present the Chipayas as savages. Without quite knowing which texts he's referring to, I attribute them to authors of years ago, prisoners of the prejudices of their age. I then bring up the changes in Chipaya and (almost) shamelessly flatter the father, sharing my impressions as to the decline of the Protestant groups and the progress of the Catholics since my last visit. Now more relaxed, he comments on my impressions and begins speaking freely, outlining the history of his missionary action.

Father Ramon is from Cochabamba. He describes himself as an active, stubborn, willfully provocative man. Very aware of the importance of his mission, he recalls the brief efforts of Father Amado, whom the Chipayas expelled from the village thirty years ago. It is not a village that lends itself to having a priest in residence. The lifestyle continues to be difficult, and the inhabitants quite unusual: he insists (despite his remarks concerning anthropological writings) on the violent and aggressive nature of the Chipayas, who nonetheless turn out to be cowards when you stand up to them. He has therefore made it his policy to firmly resist any aggression against him. The main reason is that he encountered major troubles at the beginning of his stay. Certain followers condemned him for surrounding the church and his office with a high wall, as if he wanted to appropriate the land. But it was the Protestants, especially, who did everything in their power to get rid of him. They denounced him first by accusing him of being a communist; the *sub-prefecto* of Sabaya, accompanied by a delegation, came all the way to Chipaya one day, burst into the church, interrupted the mass, and remonstrated with the priest, saying that this was a place of worship and not a site for political gatherings. The father had to go to the Bishop of Oruro, who accorded him his protection. But the story goes on. One night, they tried to set fire to his house; he kept a few traces of the damage as proof. Another night, a drunkard knocked on his door and threatened to kill him; the father went outside "almost naked" and confronted him, causing his disconcerted aggressor to run away.

Our interview is interrupted by Martin's arrival; surprised to see the priest, and no doubt intimidated, he doesn't even say hello to him. After Father Ramon leaves, I go over the story I have just heard. Martin smiles: no, the Protestants didn't try to burn down the priest's house (indeed, this kind of violence is not their style); it was some Catholics who did that! As for the drunkard who threatened to kill him, it was none other than Mariano G., a rather traditionalist Catholic whom I know well: I too had a few run-ins with him in 1974, when we were waiting for the infamous truck. What did they have against the priest? Mainly his having emptied the church of its images: Santa Ana, Santiago, Geronimo are waiting to come back. Though officially the Catechists loyally support the priest, many followers don't understand this action, which seems to them more like that of a Protestant missionary. So tensions are rife in the Catholic group, while a misunderstanding is forming between the priest and his flock.

A few days later, Father Ramon comes back to see me: now *he* wants to talk, and I invite him in once again. He can't say enough about my "gentle" manner of speaking and my "subtle" remarks. He therefore wants to ask my advice: the rivalries between the two *ayllus* disturb him, and he would like me to explain the dualist organization of the Chipayas. He is working mostly with the Aransaya moiety, where the Catholics are clearly in the majority, and this gives him a guilty conscience with respect to Manasaya, where there are still many Protestants. He wants to love each moiety equally, but his actions in the village seem unbalanced. I then learned that the gifts of charitable organizations have until now followed two parallel paths (in conformity with the dualist organization): aid to "Project Children," which is Catholic, is administered by Aransaya residents, while "World Vision," which is Protestant, is administered by those in Manasaya. World Vision, however, ended two years ago (Is this one of the rea-

sons for the shrinking Protestant population?), and
so Father Ramon envisions extending "Project Children" to the whole of the village. I encourage him in
his generosity, but put some disturbing thoughts in
his head when I prudently mention the growing
popularity of the customs, which unquestionably
have some negative aspects—a definite return to
drinking—but also bring positive change, since they
favor this unification of the village to which the father aspires.

It is true that the religious calm itself seems partial, and fragile. It is the result of a sort of equilib-
rium between two different interpretations for the
Chipayas' misfortunes (sickness, poor harvests,
etc.): either these are God's way of punishing them
for their continued attachment to the customs, or
they are brought on by the abandoned *mallkus*. It's
as if, when in doubt, religious practices are divided
up according to personal options so as to make up
for or complete one another. But isn't there a contradiction in taking precautions on several fronts
like this? Does such heterogeneity still have any
meaning?

Parties in the Pampa

SEVEN

THE SCHOOL DIRECTOR, A PLUMP LITTLE MAN,
jovial, lively, and extremely talkative, is eager to
spend time with me to discuss the history of the
Chipaya culture. Unlike the priest, he is interested
enough in the work of anthropologists to have com-
piled a collection of photocopies of documents concerning the village, and more generally the Urus.
Proud of his compilation, he invites me to his office
to show me the file: in it I find texts by Arturo Pos-
nansky and by Enrique Palavecino, and even one of
my own articles. The director flips through his file
and comments on it endlessly, lingering on the tech-
nical and linguistic aspects, addressing me as "Professor." To convince me further, he begins reading
long passages aloud, and I am surprised to find that
he stumbles just as much as the priest's assistant at
the church or as the pastor at the Pentecostal chapel.
He obviously doesn't really understand what he's
reading, but he persists, poring over all the items in
his file. How strange it is to hear my own prose
chopped up and disfigured like this.

Despite his interest in Chipaya culture (he again
refers to the project for a local museum), the director
does not have a very flattering view of the village residents. Eager to please me, he picks up the theme of 129

the savage Urus, *chullpa-puchu,* the rejects of humanity. It is a difficult mission for the teachers to "civilize" these primitive creatures. When they begin their education, the youngest students don't speak a word of Spanish; their progress is slow because they lack intelligence. As for the older ones, they are shameless: no matter how much you punish them, they mate "precociously." From the time they are twelve years old, the girls deliberately excite the boys, which is why the Chipayas reproduce "like rabbits." When I suggest that some of the villagers themselves might be trained as teachers, who would then have an easier time because of their knowledge of the Puquina language, the director categorically rejects the idea: such teachers would only retard the students further. They must be educated in the Aymara and Bolivian cultures.

The irony of the story? While the school director is a perfect example of the Aymaras' disdain for the *chullpa-puchu,* he himself is from Challacollo, a village near Oruro. The viceroy Francisco of Toledo's census indicated that Challacollo was populated entirely with Urus, who abandoned nomadism and settled there at some point during the seventeenth century, adopting the Aymara culture; their descendants lost all memory of this assimilation. At the idea that his ancestors might have been Urus, the director bursts out laughing, incredulous.

§

Aside from festival periods, the silence of the Chipaya nights, as I had always experienced them, was of an almost tangible intensity, as if accentuated by the brilliancy of the air. Now I find yet another new development: since the beginning of my stay I have been hearing strange noises almost every night—echoing footsteps, the sound of someone running, snatches of conversation, laughter, and especially the echoes of blaring music. I find this nocturnal commotion intriguing and soon learn what it's all about: it's the "youth," gathering for a party in a house in the village or in the surrounding pampa. These are fourteen- or fifteen-year-olds, adolescents who are still in junior high school. The parties, my informants say, are "very particular" in the sense that, unlike the old kind, they are private in nature and can take place at any time. The music that now pervades the nights in Chipaya, and which these young people are dancing to, is produced, I'm amused to learn, by a *grabadora* (tape recorder). Some of my many godchildren are old enough to participate in these parties: they explain to me that they are organized at different people's houses following a kind of rotation system, or sometimes at an *estancia,* outdoors. Their favorite dances are *cumbias,* especially rock! Although I have expressed a desire to join them, none of my godchildren has ever invited me to a gathering: I'm definitely too old. So I was unable to attend one of these events, which I imagine must be curious: boys in shirts and trousers, girls dressed in the traditional black tunic, bobbing up and down to rock music beneath star-lit sky in this desolate pampa.

How did these young people learn modern dances? They travel to the Chilean valleys, to the city, and listen to the radio. When I ask my godchildren what presents they want, they give me a specific list of cassettes they'd like to have. The parents are worried about these activities, which only took hold in the village four or five years ago: these kids not only dance, they also drink and get drunk as much as adults, and then get into fights! Such behavior had never been seen in Chipaya at such an early age. Those parents who also drink are full of righteous indignation, remembering their own youth: "At their age, when we were single, we didn't take part in the festivals, we didn't drink. Our parents were the ones who drank, while we watched over the animals. We only started later, after we were married!" On the morning of October 19, I learn that a meeting is being held in the *corregidor*'s office to deal with an unprecedented scandal. The previous night, two boys who had already been drinking knocked on the door of Filipe M., who owns a shop where they thought they could find jugs of liquor. They asked him to sell them some. When Filipe refused, the two boys beat him up. This adolescent aggression against an adult has the village in a state of commotion.

What is equally surprising is that the family tradition in which these adolescents were raised seems immaterial. The ones who go to parties come from both traditionalist and Evangelical or Pentecostal families with puritan morals, but they make no distinction when they gather together. Here then is another type of unification brought about by the younger generation's openness to input from the media, accompanied by dissatisfaction, even disgust, with village life. The licentious behavior of the young is perceived by the parents as provocation, rebellion: according to them, their children are possessed by a kind of "frenzy." But what frenzy? Rebellion against whom? There is no longer any tradition to reject: it was the parents' generation that abandoned the customs (or "reformed" them). Now the youth no longer believe in anything. The *mallkus?* The rituals of the past? Those outmoded beliefs are a joke, they're from another era. The Evangelical or Pentecostal religions? In the best of cases, they accompany their parents to the services, without sharing their convictions. (One factor in the decline of the Protestant groups is no doubt the adults' failure to transmit their faith to their children.) All that remains, then, among the young, is indifference tainted with confusion. What *do* they aspire to? To get away! To escape the miserable life to which people are condemned in this remote village. They dream of the riches promised by the colonization projects in the warm valleys, of the glistening comfort of the cities. Yet these adolescents are well aware of reality: they know that very few of them can leave, and that of those who do, fewer still ever attain a comfortable living. The horizon seems closed. There is no hope.

A state of anomy? A previously unheard-of phenomenon has arisen among adolescents: suicide. A half-dozen cases have been reported in the past four or five years, teenagers who killed themselves for the flimsiest of reasons. Broken hearts, of course. But also, simply, for being reprimanded by their parents. A child is reproached for going to a party, for getting drunk: "In a state of frenzy," they report, in tears, "he swallowed some poison!" Last year this misfortune struck my compadre Antonio, Gregorio's enemy brother, who is so harsh with Gregorio and so affectionate with me. His sixteen-year-old son didn't want to go to school anymore; he lectured him, trying to make him return. The young man preferred to hang himself. On All Saints' Day I naturally visit Antonio. A table is set with offerings for the soul of the deceased; in the middle, a photo of the adolescent: round head, long hair, a smile on his face. Attached to a small string, above the table, are his personal belongings: an *ira*, two pairs of pants, a jacket, a cap, "basketball shoes." A very touching scene. The family members, sitting on the floor, are plunged in silence. My three-year-old godchild is playing in a corner. Antonio offers me a tall glass of lemonade. He is not weeping, but his expression is vacant, his voice hoarse: "I'm offering you lemonade, not liquor, because he was so young. I didn't understand, I still don't understand. Maybe he's happier now. I cried so much last year. Now I cry less, I'm starting to get used to it."

EIGHT

Final Note

I WAS FINISHING THESE LINES, CONVINCED THAT they were the last I would write about Chipaya, when other echoes reached me in Paris. In early June 1991, in my office on the boulevard Raspail, I received a phone call from a traveler just back from a month in the village. Pierre Espagne, a consultant for a development project sponsored by a "nongovernmental organization," introduced himself. A curious coincidence: during his stay he was housed at the home of my compadre Antonio, whose sorrow I had shared during All Saints' Day in 1989. I thus learned the latest news from Chipaya: is this yet another epilogue to an epilogue, or an afterword and ending?

The period of appeasement that the village had enjoyed for several years turned out to be quite fragile; Chipaya is now in turmoil again. The two *ayllus,* Aransaya and Manasaya, are opposing each other because of a colonization project in the warm lands of the Alto Beni. During my last stay, I witnessed the beginnings of the conflict but didn't imagine the repercussions it would have. Lists were circulating to register heads of families interested in the project, and the Aransaya members were already reproaching Manasaya members for hoarding documents and enrolling en masse, thereby excluding all the other Chipayas from the program. Of the forty-two volunteers eventually registered, thirty-nine belong to Manasaya (or more than half the heads of family in the *ayllu*) and only three to Aransaya. Even though the departure for these colonies is not yet certain (women and children stay in the village until the reclaimed land becomes productive), a serious imbalance now affects the respective populations of the two moieties. The Manasayas' monopoly on the lands distributed in the Alto Beni is turning against them: the Aransayas, now twice as numerous in the village, are demanding an extension of their territory to the detriment of that of the other *ayllu*. It's true that this conflict is merely an inversion of the one that caused the two moieties to face off for control of the water at the beginning of the nineteenth century, when Manasaya numbered twice as many tributaries as Aransaya. But today, after so much upheaval, one of the final components inherited from the ancient order—the dualist organization—is being threatened.

Furthermore, the religious peace has finally ended. Father Ramon no longer lives in Chipaya: the hostility of a good part of his flock won out over his stubbornness, and he was virtually banished from the village. The Catholics, who had attained a dominant position, are now beginning to dwindle. On the other hand, two new Protestant sects (Baptist and Adventist) have taken root and are experiencing rapid growth, accompanying their missionary action with generous gifts. There even seem to be many young people among their followers (but parties continue nonetheless to enliven the Chipaya nights).

With the instability of groups of believers, crisscrossing from one church to another, and repeated conversions, the Chipayas' never-ending religious quest is following an ever more erratic itinerary. In the old days, people knew which customs to follow in all circumstances. Everything was precisely codified, ritual permeated all social relations, and each individual was part of an organized universe, where meaning was to be found. It is this vanished meaning that is now desperately being sought: all the codes have crumbled, the *mallkus* have disappeared, the order of the world has unraveled, and the Chipayas literally no longer know what to believe. Joining the new churches is a sign of their desire to break out of their marginal status, and to attain universality, as well as modernity, but the Chipayas, now torn between dereliction in their windswept pampa and exile in the torrid valleys, can't escape what defines them at heart: their status as *chullpa-puchu,* rejects from humanity.

Is it wrong for the ethnologist to yield to nostalgia
at seeing his area of study fall apart over the years? I
know that this desolate village, like all societies, is
being caught up in the tide of history. I spent years
studying the formation of an identity which, having had a moment of creation (toward the middle
of the eighteenth century), will certainly have an
end. The accelerated transformations that at the end
of the twentieth century are affecting not only Bolivia but the entire globe are inevitably reaching every corner of the world. Should the contributions of
modernity be limited to the introduction of the water faucet today, electricity tomorrow? Might it not
contain meaning in itself, different but equally rich
as that conferred by a world now passed?

This very passing is the crux of the matter. For
while the ethnologist begins by meddling in a society which at first is only of intellectual interest to
him, he ends up, in a just reversal of circumstances,
internalizing this object of study, made up of living
beings with whom he maintains relations of friendship or hostility, with whom he has shared every-
day joys and sorrow. While I got mixed up in the
history of Chipaya, Chipaya also got mixed up in
mine: indeed, it's a part of me that time is taking
away. What's left? Writings and memories. As Benito said, "You see, the photo is still here." He added
a "forever," of which I am less sure. Looking up,

I contemplate the large photograph that presides over my office: in the waters of Lake Coipasa, its crusts of salt twinkling with bluish reflections, a Chipaya hunter, in suspended motion, forms a tiny dark spot, lost in the grey and white immensity and overshadowed by the distant ridge of snowy mountaintops, unchanging in their beauty.

Notes

1. See Nathan Wachtel, *Le Retour des ancêtres: Les Indiens Urus de Bolivie, XXᵉ–XVIᵉ siècle. Essai d'histoire régressive* (Paris: Gallimard, 1990), 639–55.

2. *Día de la raza:* holiday celebrated October 12, instituted in Spain in 1915, then in various countries of Latin America, commemorating Christopher Columbus's discovery of America.

3. Wachtel, *Le Retour des ancêtres.*

4. *Ira:* a male Chipaya garment, a kind of poncho with fine brown and white vertical stripes.

5. *Aqsu:* the main element of female dress in Chipaya, a tunic composed of two rectangular pieces of fabric sewn together, in black or dark brown.

6. For a more detailed analysis of these terms, see Gilles Rivière, "Lik'ichiri y kharisiri: a propósito de las representaciones del 'Otro' en la sociedad aymara," *Bulletin de l'Institut français d'études andines* 20, no. 1 (1991); in the same issue there is a general presentation of the theme of the *pishtako* by Antoinette Molinié-Fioravanti, as well as her article "Sebo bueno, indio muerto: La estructura de una creencia andina." I am sincerely grateful to Antoinette Molinié-Fioravanti and Gilles Rivière for sharing their texts (still unpublished at the time of this writing) with me, and allowing me to cite them.

7. According to Jan Szeminski, "Un Kuraka, un dios, y una historia ('Relación de antiguedades de este reymo del Pirú' por don Juan Santa Cruz Pachucuti Yamqui Salca Maygua)," *Antropologia social e Historia,* no. 2, July, 1987, 12–27.

8. On this point, see especially Molinié-Fioravanti, "Sebo bueno, indio muerto" (note 6 above).

9. The description presented in this paragraph is drawn from information gathered by Efaín Morote Best, "El de-

gollador (Nakaq)," *Tradición* 2 no. 4 (1952): 67–91, reprinted in *Aldeas submergidas: Cultura popular y sociedad en los Andes* (Cuzco, 1988) 153–77.

10. Cristobal de Molina ("del Cuzco"), "Relación de las fábulas y ritos de los Incas" [1572], *Colección de libros y documentos referentes a la Historia del Perú*, series 1, vol. 1 (Lima, 1916), 97.

11. Ibid., 98.

12. Ibid., 98–99.

13. Ibid., 99.

14. Ibid., 97–98.

15. Archives générales des Indes (Séville), Audiencìa Lima 316, "Informaciones de servicios" de Cristobal de Albornoz, notebook from 1571, f. 16 r.–16 v. and f. 33 r.

16. See Rafael Varón Gabai, "El Taki Onqoy: las raíces andinas de un fenómeno colonial," in *El retorno de las huacas,* edited by Luis Millones (Lima, IEP, 1990), 375–77.

17. Felipe Guaman Poma de Ayala, *El primer Nueva corónica y buen gobierno* [1615], edited by John V. Murra and Rolena Adorno, (Mexico City, 1980), 282.

18. Pablo José de Arriaga, *La extirpación de la idolatría en el Perú* [1621], BAE, vol. 209 (Madrid, 1968), 208.

19. P. Fr. Joseph García de la Concepción, *Historia bethlehemitica, vida exemplar y admirable del venerable siervo de Dios y Padre Pedro de San Joseph Betancur, fundador de el regular instituto de Bethlehem en las Indias Occidentales; frutos sinculares de su fecundo espíritu y sucesos varios de est religion* (Séville, 1723), cited by Best (note 9 above), 168–70.

20. Ibid.

21. Ibid.

22. See Efraín Morote Best, "Addenda," in *Aldeas submergidas* (note 9 above), 357–58.

23. Julio Caro Baroja, *Ensayo sobre la literatura de cordel*

(Madrid, 1969), 156–57; see also Lilia Pérez González, "Algunas consideraciones sobre el sacamantecas y el chupasangres," *Papeles de Son Armadans* no. 163 (1978): 186–87.

24. González, "Algunas consideraciones," 187.

25. Víctor Lis Quiben, *La medicina popular en Galicia* ([1949] Madrid, 1980), 308, cited by Best (note 9 above), 358.

26. Best (note 9 above), 358.

27. Ibid.; José María Arguedas, "Cuentos mágico-realistas y canciones de fiesta tradicional del Valle del Mantaro, Provincias de Jauja y Concepcion," *Folklore americano* 1, no. 1 (1953): 101–93.

28. See Juan Ansion and Eudosio Sifuentes, "La imajen popular de la violencia, a traves de los relatos de degolladores," in *Pishtacos: De verdugos a sacajos,* edited by Juan Ansion (Lima, 1989), 72–75.

29. Ibid., 75–77.

30. Ibid., 99–100.

31. Carlos Iván Degregori, "Entre los fuegos de Sendero y el Ejércity: Regreso de los 'Pishtacos,'" in *Pishtacos* (note 28 above), 109–14; Abilio Vergara Figueroa and Freddy Ferrúa Carrasco, "Ayacucho: de nuevo los degolladores," in ibid., 123–34.

32. Gastón Antonio Zapata, "Sobre ojos y pishtacos," in *Pishtacos* (note 28 above), 137–40; Emilio Rojas Rimachi, "Los 'sacaojos'" el miedo y la cólera," ibid., 141–47; Eudosio Sifuentes, "La continuidad de la historia de los pishtacos en los 'robaojos' de hoy," ibid., 149–54.

33. See Rimachi (note 32 above), 145.

34. See Gilles Rivière (note 6 above).

35. Ibid.

36. Ibid.

37. See Nathan Wachtel (note 1 above), 633–34.

Glossary

Alcalde: the most important *cargo* or post, both civil and religious, exercised in Chipaya within the framework of the *ayllu.*

Alsa: ceremonial meal offered by the *pasante* to the inhabitants of a village on the occasion of a saint's or a *mallku*'s feast day.

Aqsu (or *Urko*): the principal element of female dress in Chipaya—a tunic, in black or dark brown, composed of two rectangular pieces of fabric sewn together.

Ayllu: the basic unit of social organization, defined by the territory and by familial relationships, and overlapping, in Chipaya, with the moiety.

Cargo: includes a variety of civic responsibilities, from assuming certain posts (see *Alcade,* above) to sponsoring religious festivals, etc.

Chica: beer made of corn.

Chullpas: beings who, according to the creation myth, inhabited the earth before the appearance of the sun.

Chullpa-puchu: "rejects of the *chullpas,*" an insult addressed to the Chipayas by the Aymara Indians.

Chuño: a potato preserved by dehydration in the frost.

Compadre: people linked by *compadrazgo,* or ritual godparenthood, whereby the parents of a child and the child's godparents become co-parents, calling each other *compadre.*

Compadrazgo: see *Compadre.*

Corregidor: in Chipaya, the administrative director of the canton.

Estancia: in Chipaya, designates the clusters of houses that form hamlets and are distributed among arable portions of the territory.

Faena: collective work in the service of the community.

Huaca: sacred site, sacred object, divine entity, etc.

Ira: Chipaya male garment, a kind of poncho with fine brown and white vertical stripes.

Kamayo: "guardian of the fields," designated each year to watch over the cultivated areas.

Kharisiri: figure generally represented as a white man who extracts the fat or the blood of the Indians at dusk or at night, after having plunged his victims into a deep sleep.

Kulli: ground black corn (ritual offering).

Lik'ichiri: see Kharisiri.

Llumpaja: ground white corn (ritual offering).

Mallku: in Chipaya, designates chthonian divinities whose spirit is supposed to reside in cone-shaped monuments made of adobe and dried earth one to two meters in height.

Mesa: ritual table bearing the offerings to the divinities; in Chipaya, it generally consists of one piece of cloth laid with thirty-six shallow cups containing the various ingredients that the *sukachiri* sprinkles on the ground as a drink offering.

Nakaq: see Kharisiri.

Pasante: person designated each year to sponsor the following year's celebration of a saint or a *mallku*.

Pishtako: see Kharisiri.

Samiris: divinities of strong chthonian character who protect animals (both domestic and wild); originally flat stones of indeterminate form that were buried beneath the *mallkus*.

Sebario: mineral powder (ritual offering).

Sukachiri: specialized officiant, charged with executing the ritual during the festival of a saint or a *mallku*.

Taki: dance, chant (secular or religious).

Tishñe: ritual cycle formerly celebrated in Chipaya in honor of the divinities that protect the lakes and the cultivated lands.

Yatiri: sorcerer, or, more generally, diviner, healer, etc.

Index